INTRODUCING AUSTRIA

STUDIES IN AUSTRIAN LITERATURE, CULTURE, AND THOUGHT

Lonnie Johnson

INTRODUCING AUSTRIA

A Short History

Ariadne Press
270 Goins Court
Riverside, California 92507

Published by
Österreichischer Bundesverlag Gesellschaft m.b.H.
Vienna, 1987
ISBN: 978-0-929497-03-7

Table of Contents

Preface

This "guide of sorts" is for people whose needs and interests go beyond the ones met by traditional guidebooks. Although it does have some suggestions about things to do and see in Austria (in an appendix "Typically Provincial – Tips for Touring"), it is not an alphabetically organized compilation of details about Austria's attractions: the breathtaking sites, historical landmarks, and beautiful monuments which are the composite parts of Austria's image. Most guidebooks use these highlights as points of orientation, and this sometimes inadvertently creates the impression that Austria is a cross between a charming Alpine resort and a fascinating open-air museum. This guide of sorts uses different criteria as points of reference: events, attitudes, and traditions which can be described as attributes of the Austrian idea.

The first half of this book deals with Austria before 1918 and is basically a series of illustrations. Each chapter and subchapter approaches Austria's diverse, thousand-year-old heritage from a different perspective in an attempt to illuminate some of its essential features. Therefore, readers should not expect a straightforward historical synopsis, but rather be prepared to see how the pieces of the Austrian mosaic fit together. The second half of this book deals with Austria's turbulent history since 1918 and intends to bring readers up to date. Both halves together should give readers a feeling for the continuity and change of the Austrian idea.

This book has been written by a foreigner for other foreigners. Nevertheless, it would be difficult for me even to begin to list all of the Austrians who have contributed to it in one way or another. If they recognize their contributions, I am glad and thank them; if they do not, it merely testifies to the differences between self-perception and foreign observation, and I thank them, too. Needless to say, I have tried to present a balanced picture of Austria, and I have attempted to avoid the extremes towards which Austrians of different temperaments occasionally gravitate when they write about Austria: obliviously self-righteous optimism or masochistically critical pessimism.

Austria

DANUBE

FEDERAL REPUBLIC of GERMANY

Lake
Constance

Bregenz

Vorarlberg

LIECHTEN-
STEIN

Inn

Innsbruck

Tyrol

Salzb

Brenner
Pass

SWITZERLAND

ITALY

In particular, I am indebted to Siegwald Ganglmair and David Steele for reading the entire manuscript and making a series of valuable criticisms and suggestions, as well as to Inge and Friedl Lehne for their helpful remarks on the first four chapters. Completing this project would have been impossible without the help of my wife, Monika – the best reason I have for being in Austria.

This book is dedicated to my parents who, well over a decade ago, supported the idea of having their son study abroad for a year in Austria, and unfortunately have not seen enough of him ever since.

Lonnie Johnson

9

Introduction: Are the Hills Alive with the Sound of Music?

The Sound of Music has perhaps done more to popularize Austria in the past decades than anything else. Julie Andrews sang her way through the breathtaking landscapes and the quaint scenery of the province and city of Salzburg, motifs which Technicolor captured so well. This combination of music and melodrama was a great success at the box office, in the English-speaking world in particular. The longevity of the impression created by this film is best documented by the fact that the "Sound of Music Tour" in Salzburg is still going strong even though the film, made in 1964, is already a classic of sorts. Austrians themselves did not particularly care for the film. They thought it was kitschy and sentimental, at least in a manner that did not appeal to their own peculiar streak of kitsch and sentimentality.

The popular image of Austria in the world today is not a reflection of great political deeds or astounding economic achievements. On the contrary, it can be reduced to two broad sets of associations which mirror the beauty of Austria's physical landscape and the richness of its cultural landscape: one of them is Alpine – mountains and music; the other is Viennese – waltzes and whipped cream.

For some people the contours of the Alpine associations are not quite sharp enough. Western Austria is frequently confused with Switzerland even though the Winter Olympics have been held in Innsbruck twice. Indeed, the mountains are scenic in both countries. The Swiss Alps are a bit higher and more expensive to ski in than their Austrian counterparts, but people inevitably tend to imagine the same things: in winter, mountain chalets and skiers waist-deep in fields of untouched powder snow; in summer, snow-covered peaks and a cow peacefully grazing on the mountainside with a clinking bell around its neck. Fresh air and fun or peace and quiet, as you like. Other people tend to confuse Austria with Bavaria – the brass band, *Lederhosen*, and beer cliché.

The fact that these areas are frequently confused with each other

*Austrian associations:
Skiers in the
Arlberg region...*

is understandable because they have a number of characteristics in common. Exaggerating their similarities, however, involves underestimating essential differences in national traditions, customs, and temperaments. Calling a Tyrolean Bavarian or Swiss is an indiscretion that borders on insult for all parties involved. It is like confusing England, Scotland, and Wales, or the USA and Canada.

There is also occasional nominal confusion between Australia and Austria or Vienna and Venice. The two countries, well over 10,000 miles apart, are separated in most dictionaries only by a few seldom used adjectives like australopithecine. American mail sorters in particular have a knack for periodically rerouting letters to Austria via Sydney.

The two cities, on the other hand, can be distinguished in terms of their canals: Venice's are grand; Vienna's are solely for sewage. The Viennese canals' only real claim to fame is that they provided part of the subterranean setting for Orson Welles' mysterious escapes and

... and waltzing couples at the opening of the Vienna State Opera's annual "Opernball," the high point of the ball season.

final demise in a post-World War II espionage film, *The Third Man*. Needless to say, visitors to Austria and Vienna arrive expecting neither kangaroos nor gondolas.

Just like any other country, Austria employs a number of professional image-makers: an Austrian Cultural Institute can be found in many major foreign cities; trade and industry have their representatives in major business centers; and the Austrian National Tourist Office is also well represented throughout the world. The Tourist Office is undoubtedly the most successful promoter of Austrian trademarks. Promising relaxation and refinement, Austria's mountains-and-music image is popular, but market researchers have to identify other target groups, too: singles, families, the retired, experienced and inexperienced travellers, people interested in sports or culture, etc. Therefore, there are many different Austrian "packages" on the market. The country tries to be all things to all people.

Nevertheless, certain obligatory sights and attractions seem to prevail. In order to save tourists' time and give him the most for his money in Vienna, for example, someone once suggested training the Vienna Choir Boys to ride the white stallions of the Spanish Riding School. The performance could be held in the park of Schönbrunn Palace, where vendors could sell *Sachertorte* to the spectators.

The Austrian author Hans Weigel once remarked that some Austrians feel about Mozart and Strauss the same way Saudi Arabians feel about oil. If culture is an Austrian natural resource, then tourism seems to be a trade dealing in *Gemütlichkeit,* a warm, cosy, friendly experience. Tourism is, however, one of Austria's most important industries. The prosperity of entire regions and whole branches of the service economy depends on a rather simple indicator which is watched as closely as the Dow-Jones average: the number of beds filled. Austria has over one million beds for guests in accommodations ranging from private bed-and-breakfasts to luxury class hotels. Some 14 million foreigners visit the country each year: two tourists for every Austrian.

Tourism is important for the Austrian economy because the country imports more than it exports, and the income from tourism acts as an export replacement to offset a negative balance of trade. In other words, instead of selling Austrian commodities outside of the country, Austria depends on tourists to bring foreign currency into the country which makes Austria one of Austria's best "exports." The Austrian gross earnings per capita related to tourism are by far the highest in Europe. They have consistently been around $ 600 per capita in recent years, and there are seven million Austrians. That is a lot of whipped cream.

These simple facts and figures indicate why tourism is so important to Austria, but it is misleading to confuse Austria with the commercial image professional promoters have created to market Austria to non-Austrians. This image is so pronounced and one-sided that the official representatives of Austria feel that it needs to be corrected. In 1985, for example, the Austrian federal government published a book on the "other" Austria, the one which diplomats in the Ministry of Foreign Affairs are interested in promoting. Dealing with various aspects of Austrian industry, science, politics, and foreign relations, it was distributed as a gift to 5,000 influential Americans to let them know what Austria really is like. Its title, *The Sound of Austria,* enticed American readers with a common association, but this type of promotion is necessary because the touristic cliché overwhelms everything else. Instead of mountains-and-music, Austrian officials would prefer Austria, the land of low unemployment, high productivity, quality products, social welfare, and circumspect neutrality. They have a tough job because the Alps and Mozart are much more prominent trademarks.

Austrians are extremely image-conscious. They do not like to see their country misrepresented as some kind of touristic playground, but this image is enduring. Austria is too small to make international headlines unless a scandal attracts the kind of attention the lesser-known merits of the country cannot. Scandals are the only thing that can really smudge Austria's cheery touristic image. In other words, bad press is often the only kind of international press Austria gets.

For example, the United States has accused Austria of being the site of illegal transfers of Western high technology, which can be used for military purposes, to the Soviet Union. The fact that many recent espionage affairs involved Americans meeting their Soviet contacts in Vienna has contributed further to a dubious cloak-and-dagger image of unreliability, reinforced by the latest James Bond film (with Timothy Dalton and Maryam d'Abo), The Living Daylights.

Then there was the wine scandal. A handful of dishonest vintners recently doctored their wines with diethylene glycol, an antifreeze additive that "improved" the taste of low-quality wine. All over the world, countries forbade the sale of Austrian wines until the doctored wines could be traced, and in Japan some stores immediately took Australian wines off the shelves. This incident damaged Austria's reputation for quality and honesty. (A consolation was that physicians discovered that the amounts of diethylene glycol used in the doctored wines were no more damaging to the people who drank them than the alcohol in the wine. Both toxic substances are bad for the liver, kidneys, and central nervous system.)

Austria also has had periodic episodes involving old Nazis. When Italy released Walter Reder, the last Nazi war criminal it detained, to Austria in 1985, Austrian officials bungled the entire affair and created the impression that he was practically being officially welcomed home. As bad as this was, it was merely a prelude to the so-called "Waldheim affair."

During his campaign for president in 1986, information about Kurt Waldheim's activities in World War II came out which he had not previously and publicly offered. In accusations that filled international headlines for weeks, Waldheim, a low-ranking officer in the

German Army, was portrayed as everything from a Nazi to a war criminal who had escaped justice. Austria has never received such extensive coverage from the international media.

Even though many of the allegations made against Waldheim have remained inconclusive or have been proved false, the Waldheim affair added a new dimension to Austria's international image. Austrians look back to the good old days when their only real problem was the mountains-and-music cliché; now they have to deal with the mountains-and-music-and-Nazis cliché.

Even though mountains, music, and Nazis are treated in this book, it does not deal exclusively with these topics. This book has been written for people who want a critical introduction to Austria, the Austria behind the clichés and bad press. As a foreigner, the author is fully aware of the problems involved in this type of venture. The Austrian writer Karl Heinrich Waggerl once observed: "The Austrian loves his country, even dearly, although he constantly complains, and the better he feels, the more he complains. However, he would be deeply offended if an outsider were somehow to agree with him."

In order to understand Austria, one has to go back much further than the advent of modern Austria in 1918. Therefore, the first half of this book offers a panoramic view of what Austria once was, a small medieval realm which, in the course of centuries, became a Central European empire, before turning to how Austria became what it is today: a small state with a big history.

1. What is Austria?

Everyone knows where this small Central European state is: in the Alps. Never satisfied with the obvious, geographers feel compelled to point out the non-alpine characteristics of the country, such as the plateau of the Bohemian Massif north of the Danube River, the Danube Valley north of the Alps, or perhaps the fact that the Hungarian Plain begins in Eastern Austria. Political scientists, never satisfied with mere topographical descriptions, stress the fact that Austria is a federal republic with nine provinces. It shares borders with seven other European states which can be subdivided into two to four distinct socio-economic or political categories. Neither of these kinds of definition help answer a more important question: "Why is Austria where it is?" This, in turn, leads to a more complicated inquiry: "Where and what has Austria been?"

There are two basically different ways of looking at the role Austria has played in Europe, and they are related to the most obvious features of Austria's landscape. Pessimists see the natural barriers, the mountains and the rivers, and optimists see the more communicative features of the same – the passes and the valleys. The validity of each of these perspectives has shifted back and forth throughout the ages. Austria has separated all of the geopolitical points of the compass – North from South and East from West – but it has also periodically joined or even reconciled these opposites. Today it seems to be able to do both equally well.

The Borderland

Some 80,000 to 150,000 years ago, the nomadic hunters of the Stone Age regularly sought refuge in the natural shelters which the caves of the Alps provided. They probably had no idea what a border was. Turning Austria into a borderland was an achievement of a higher degree of civilization.

From 15 B.C. to 9 B.C., the Romans occupied the Alps and regions south of the Danube. In the West, the provinces of Vorarlberg and Tyrol today, the indigenous tribes put up fierce resistance and had to be "civilized" by force before the Roman province of *Raetia* could be founded. (Some people think that the residents of these provinces have never lost their tribal character.) The Roman province of *Noricum*, already well-known in those days for its exports of salt and iron, evidently was established peacefully and encompassed most of the rest of Austria south of the Danube with the exception of *Pannonia*, the easternmost part of contemporary Austria. The foundations of many Austrian cities as well as the routes of some of today's roads go back to these times, and the Romans were the first to use the thermal baths found in many Austrian spas. In spite of the rather high degree of civilization reached in these provinces, they were literally and figuratively at the end of the Roman world nonetheless.

After failing to subdue the Germanic tribes living north of the Danube and east of the Rhine, the Romans decided in the course of the first century to build a chain of fortifications along these two rivers to protect their empire. They erected a series of watchtowers and camps along the southern bank of the Danube. (Vienna, for example, was later built literally on top of the Roman camp of *Vindobona*.) This chain of fortifications, called the *Limes*, was not like the Great Wall of China. On the contrary, the camps, which were about 10 miles apart, provided bases of operation, and the troops, which were rather sparsely deployed, were supposed to prevent enemies from crossing the Danube or pursue them if they did. In the long run, they did neither particularly well. Occasionally barbarian tribes broke into the provinces to pillage and plunder, and the frequency of these intrusions from the North and the East increased as the Roman Empire declined. By the end of the fourth century, the Roman provinces had effectively ceased to exist.

During the Great Migrations, the former Roman provinces assumed a role which contemporary Austria has readopted; they served as one of Europe's most important lands of transit from North to South and East to West. Today's hordes of camera-carrying tourists follow the routes of the sword-swinging Goths and Huns. The importance of the Danube Valley is apparent to anyone who travels to Vienna from the West. The route from Vienna to Venice is hardly any different by car or rail today than it was over a thousand years ago on horse or foot; after crossing the Semmering Pass some 60 miles southwest of Vienna, a series of river valleys (the Mürz, Mur, Gurk, Drau, and Gail) provide practically direct access to Yugoslavia and Italy. Last but not least, the Inn Valley and the Brenner Pass south of Innsbruck make Tyrol one of the most convenient places to cross the Alps. These thoroughfares have always been economically and strategically important, and they are even more so today in spite of the obvious benefits of tunnel technology.

The Great Migrations created a political and military vacuum in Austria which both the East and the West aspired to fill in the course of the 8th century. The most important area of contention was the Danube Valley east of the Enns River, part of today's provincial border between Upper and Lower Austria, and west of two Danube tributaries: in the northeast, the March River, the Czechoslovak border today, and in the southeast, the Leitha River just west of the contemporary Hungarian border. The area in between was a buffer zone or no-man's-land of sorts which provided part of the setting for the most famous German medieval epic, *Das Nibelungenlied,* which Richard Wagner adopted as part of the basis for his 19th-century operatic dramatization of Germanic heroism.

While nomadic Mongolians called Avars settled in the East, Charlemagne established the Holy Roman Empire in the West. After a series of battles, Charlemagne decisively defeated the Avars at the end of the 8th century, and then he established a series of *Marken* – in Old German, *Mark* meant province as well as borderland – which were designed to secure the borders of the empire. From this point on, strong impulses for settling and Christianizing these territories came from Bavaria. For example, some of Austria's oldest churches and monasteries were founded by the German diocese of Passau. Bavarian pioneers gradually displaced the Slavs indigenous to the Danube Valley and the Alps, and they established a sphere of German influence contested by Slavs in the North and various nomadic tribes in the East.

The eastern border did not hold for long. Around 900, another combative nomadic people from the East, the Magyars, ancestors of the Hungarians, overran the eastern provinces and plundered in Germany, France, Spain, and Italy before settling down on the Hungarian Plain. They established a sphere of influence which reached to the Enns River. (The only other time in history when the Enns assumed this function of an eastern border was after World War II. From 1945 to 1955 it was part of the demarcation line between the

19

Detail from a painting of the "Babenbergs' Dynastic Tree" in the monastery of Klosterneuburg, 1497: Friedrich II's fatal fall (left foreground) and Vienna (background).

American and Soviet zones of occupation in Austria.) It was not until the Battle of Lechfeld near Augsburg in 955 that the Germans under King Otto I defeated the Magyars. The fact that this battle took place deep inside German territory shows how fluid and unstable the frontiers were in those days.

The history of Austria as a political and territorial concept began in 976 when the victorious King Otto entrusted a noble German family, the Babenbergs, with the task of consolidating and ruling a *Mark* in the Danube Valley. It was a common medieval practice for a king to give his vassal the right to rule a territory and demand allegiance in return. This event bound the name and fate of Austria to a succession of twelve Babenbergs for the next 270 years. Shortly after the Babenbergs began their rule, the name Austria appears for the first time, in a church document dated 996, as "the region commonly called *Ostarrichi*." This name was apparently derived from *oster* (eastern) and *richi* (*Reich*, kingdom or realm).

The Babenbergs accomplished the task of consolidating their holdings and securing the eastern border. They moved their residence down the Danube five times between 984 and 1156, starting in Melk and finally settling in Vienna. By the end of the 12th century, they had gained control of territories as far north as today's Czechoslovak border and as far east as the March and Leitha rivers. In the South, they acquired the *Mark* of Styria. They had to defend these territories from the Bohemians and Hungarians, and today some of the most visible reminders of the early years of expansion are the castles or ruins which dot the countryside in the provinces of Lower Austria and Styria. Often built so that their occupants could see from one to the next, they were watchposts, signal towers, lordly residences, places of refuge, and border markers all at the same time.

The last Babenberg, Friedrich II, was called "the Quarrelsome," and he was killed by the Hungarians in 1246 in a battle related to a border dispute. His death shows how unchivalrous knightly combat often was on the eastern frontier. While he was pursuing a group of fleeing Hungarians, his horse was fatally wounded and fell on top of him. The enemy returned, surrounded and killed him, then stripped him of his armor. Friedrich left neither children nor a designated successor behind, so Austria was a realm without a ruler. After his death, nothing less than the hegemony of Central Europe was at stake. The kings of Bohemia and Hungary immediately made their claims to the vacant throne.

According to medieval conventions, rulers had the right to dispose of the lands and titles of their subordinate vassals if those vassals did not have any legitimate heirs. The Babenbergs, as dukes of Austria, were the vassals of the German king, and after Friedrich II's death Austria technically became the property of the German king. These fine points did not seem to interest the King of Bohemia, Ottokar, who was married to a Babenberg princess. He took control of Austria shortly after the last Babenberg died, and he ruled it as if it were his own for almost 30 years. In 1273, the newly elected German king, a nobleman with holdings in Switzerland and southwestern Germany, Rudolph von Habsburg, decided to assert his royal rights

An illustration from a medieval manuscript on the art of war: defending a
castle by throwing stones.

and claimed Austria for himself. Hardly welcomed warmly by the Viennese, Rudolph's entry into the city was preceded by a siege in 1276. Shortly thereafter, Rudolph defeated Ottokar in one of the largest medieval battles in Europe – there were some 30,000 troops on each side – and Bohemian aspirations died with Ottokar on the battlefield in the Marchfeld northeast of Vienna. Ottokar's death and Rudolph's victory mark the end of a thirty year interregnum and the beginning of over six centuries of Habsburg rule in Austria.

The Bulwark

The modest Babenberg holdings provided the Habsburgs with the foundations for an empire, and the Habsburgs' acquisition of the rest of Austria started from the lowlands in the East and moved into the Alps in the West. Unusually enough, the Austrian Alps have never served as an international frontier, but the various ranges, mountains, and valleys within the Alps have always provided a series of inner-Austrian barriers which have naturally defined regions. In the Middle Ages, for example, the Alps contributed to the viability of smaller medieval realms in western Austria.

The Habsburgs' conquest of the Alpine territories consequently involved overcoming political obstacles which frequently corresponded to physical ones. It is also important to note that Austria's western provinces were initially independent realms with their own lords as well as political and cultural traditions that predated Habsburg rule by centuries. Geography is still one of the keys to understanding the history and mentality of Austria's western provinces. Naturally separated and defined by the Alps, each region developed fundamentally different and autonomous traditions. The Tyroleans, for example, were Tyrolean before the introduction of Habsburg rule made them "Austrian," and they did not lose their sense of independence and self-sufficiency as Tyroleans by becoming subjects of the Habsburgs.

Although the term *dominium Austriae*, an "Austrian domain," appears in a document in the early 14th century, the Habsburgs' long and complicated process of consolidation, which was based on conquest and contract, was periodically interrupted by internal discord and external challenges. By 1500 the Habsburg territories were

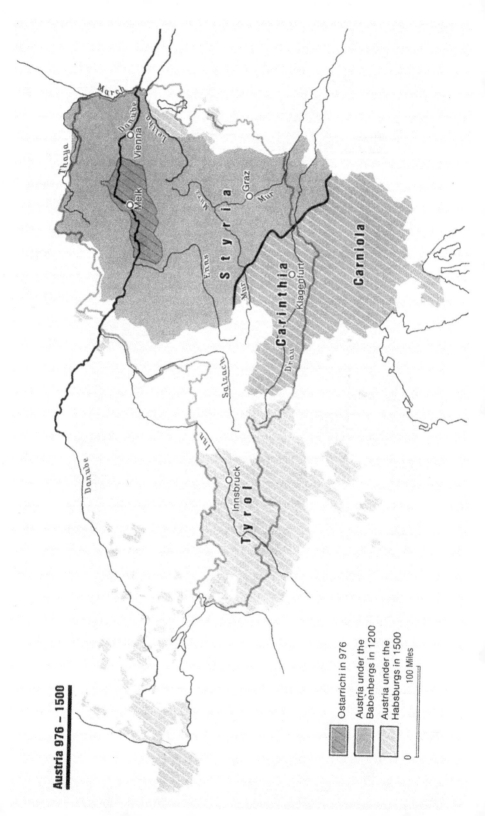

Austria 976 – 1500

Ostarrichi in 976

Austria under the
Babenbergs in 1200

Austria under the
Habsburgs in 1500

0   100 Miles

Tyrol
Innsbruck
Inn
Salzach

Carinthia
Klagenfurt
Drau

Carniola

Styria
Graz
Mur
Mur

Enns
Mur

Danube
Vienna
Melk
Danube
Leitha
March
Thaya

somewhat larger than Austria is today, but Austria was far from being a state in the modern sense of the word at that time. It was part of a conglomeration of hereditary lands known as the House of Habsburg or the House of Austria. The name for the dynasty and the realm became practically interchangeable in the course of time.

Many of the Habsburgs' future territorial gains were made by marrying at the altar instead of fighting on the battlefield. This practice does not imply that the Habsburgs did not have to do their fair share of fighting, nor does it mean that they were an especially attractive or amorous group of rulers. On the contrary, one of the family's most pronounced physical features was a long, sometimes hooked nose, and they have a reputation for being rather conscientious husbands instead of great lovers. However, marriage was primarily a diplomatic institution among the rulers of Europe in those days, and the Habsburgs married well. A famous saying captured the Habsburg policy of international intermarriage: *Bella gerant alii, tu felix Austria nube.* (Let the others fight wars; you, lucky Austria, marry.)

This proverbial wisdom refers especially to the diplomatic matchmaking of Maximilian I and illustrates how Austria began to assume an increasingly international character. In 1477, Maximilian married Maria, the heiress to Burgundy, a realm which stretched from eastern France up to the Flemish coast and enjoyed a reputation as the cultural pearl of Europe. Then he arranged a marriage between his son, Philip, and Juana, the heiress to the diverse Spanish holdings of Castile and Aragon, in 1496. (If you have ever wondered why the Spanish Riding School is in Vienna instead of Madrid, this is one of the reasons.) Finally, his pièce de résistance involved the double engagement of his grandchildren to the children of Ladislas, the King of Hungary and Bohemia. When the preliminary negotiations took place in 1506, one of Maximilian's grandsons, either Karl or Ferdinand, who were eight and three at the time, was promised to Ladislas' daughter, Anna, also a mere child. Maximilian's newly born granddaughter, Maria, was reserved as the bride for a not-yet-born son of Ladislas. This entire arrangement was formalized with a ceremonious double engagement in Vienna's St. Stephen's Cathedral in 1516 and concluded a few years later when the adolescent Habsburgs, Ferdinand and Maria, married their equally young Hungarian partners, Anna and Louis.

To make a rather long and complicated story short, the eldest

25

grandson of Maximilian, Karl V, embodied the results of three generations of marital diplomacy. From his grandfather, he inherited the Austrian lands; from his grandmother, Burgundy; and from his parents, the Spanish holdings, which included southern Italy and much of the New World. Seeing that this was a bit too much to manage all at one time, Karl agreed to concede the Austrians holdings to his younger brother, Ferdinand, who, in fact, was left with the second-choice lands. In those days, the holdings in the West seemed much more promising than those in the East, but in the long run the Austrian line of the Habsburgs did better than the Spanish line. The former ruled until 1918 but the latter died out in 1700.

The unexpected but not necessarily unwelcome death of Louis II, the King of Bohemia and Hungary and Ferdinand's brother-in-law from the famous double marriage, completely changed the prospects for the Habsburgs in the East. Louis was killed in a battle with the Turks in the swamps of southern Hungary in 1526, and he left no male heir to take his place. With the death of Louis II, Ferdinand assumed a twofold task. On the one hand, be became the King of Bohemia and Hungary (in addition to being the Archduke of Austria), and this provided him with the basis for a much larger Central European empire. On the other hand, he assumed responsibility for defending Europe against the Turks, who in the course of the previous centuries had conquered practically the entire Balkan Peninsula. They occupied Hungary even before Ferdinand had a chance to rule there and began threatening Austria itself.

Under these circumstances, Austria became a bulwark of Christianity against the Orient. Though the intensity of the conflict ebbed and flowed, the Turks represented a permanent threat to Austria and Europe for the next 150 years. They besieged Vienna in 1529 and again in 1683, and had the fortified city fallen, the course of Austrian history as well as Western civilization would have been different. The Turks planned on turning Vienna's St. Stephen's Cathedral into a mosque, and they certainly would not have stopped there. In between the sieges, the Turks periodically raided Austria's southern and eastern provinces, renewing the defensive function of the old medieval castles or fortified cities in those areas. One contemporary reminder of those days is the Armory in Graz, the provincial capital of Styria, which houses the world's largest collection of 16th and 17th century weapons.

After the second Turkish siege of Vienna in 1683, Austrian, Ger-

An engraving of the Turkish Siege of Vienna in 1683: in the background, flanked by Turkish tents, the system of trenches the Turks dug to reach Vienna's fortifications, the besieged city, and the Danube.

man, and Polish troops soundly defeated the Turks, and the Habsburgs made enormous territorial gains in the East and the South in the process of expelling the Turkish threat. In the following decades, they gained control of Hungary, where they finally asserted their title as king after 160 years of claiming it in absentia, as well as vast stretches of territory in contemporary northern Yugoslavia and Rumania.

If the Turks represented the most dangerous external threat to Austria in the 16th and 17th centuries, the rise of Protestantism during the same period was an internal menace for the Habsburgs as Catholic lords. A bulwark of Christianity in the conflicts with the Turks, the Habsburgs simultaneously became a bulwark of Catholicism in the course of the religious and political conflicts among Christians themselves – the Reformation and the Counter-Reformation. The teachings of Luther fell on fertile ground in Austria, and by 1550 the great majority of the Habsburgs' subjects were Protestant. In response to these intolerable developments, the Habsburgs spearheaded the counteroffensive of the Catholic Church in Central Europe and pursued a ruthless policy of conversion, a common and sanctioned practice for lords in those days. The Turks, as a mutual enemy, helped the quarrelling Christians periodically settle their differences as a matter of necessity, but in the long run Austria was successfully reconverted into a Catholic land. The fact that Austria is over eighty percent Catholic today is fundamentally a result of the Counter-Reformation, and the prolificity of Baroque churches and monasteries throughout the country testifies to the fervor of the Catholic Church's campaign.

It is difficult to overestimate the impact of the Counter-Reformation and Baroque culture on Austria, phenomena which were Spanish and Italian in origin. Many of the distinctions between Austrians and Germans have something to do with the fact that the southern "Germans" – Bavarians as well as Austrians – were reconverted to Baroque Catholicism whereas the northern Germans remained Protestant. The Roman Catholic Church showed its strict and dogmatic face in Austria throughout the ages in confessional questions, but it also contributed to transmitting certain attitudes or values which are more Mediterranean than they are Germanic. Gemütlichkeit may be defined as a peculiarly Alpine or trans-Alpine version of the types of attitudes found in Mediterranean Catholic culture; the Protestant work ethic was definitely not an Austrian invention.

28

The political and religious conflicts of those days also left their mark on the Austrian way of looking at the world. The permanent threat of the Turks (combined with the inadequacy of defenses in many cases) merely reconfirmed Austrians' belief that their lives were in the hands of the Lord, and the periodically ruthless manner the Habsburgs used to deal with their subjects also made them realize that their lives were also in their lords' hands. Proverbial Austrian traits like equanimity at its best or fatalism at its worst, a belief in some kind of preordained order but not in predestination, or a feeling for the dramatic and tragic aspects of life, are in many respects remnants of the days when Austria was a bulwark of Christianity and became a bulwark of Catholicism.

The Heart of Europe

In the course of the 18th century, Austrian conflicts shifted from the center of the Habsburg Empire to its peripheries. The series of wars and conclusions of peace which led to gains for the Habsburgs here and losses there is a long and complicated story in itself; however, by the middle of the 18th century, the Habsburg Empire covered most of Central Europe and northern Italy, and the Habsburg responsible for defending and consolidating these increasingly diverse holdings is one of the most popular figures in Austrian history, Maria Theresia.

As the only female regent in the Habsburgs' long dynastic line, Maria Theresia was an exception, but she also was an exceptional ruler. After the death of her father, Charles VI, in 1740, she defended the Habsburgs' hereditary claim to a unified and indivisible empire by fighting a series of wars with Prussia, Bavaria, and France, each of which either wanted to make territorial gains at her expense or questioned the legitimacy of her right to succession altogether. Maria Theresia was a successful woman in a man's world and a mother of sixteen children who showed a great deal of maternal concern not only for her own offspring but also for the well-being of all her peoples. She was an absolute ruler but also an enlightened reformer concerned with improving public administration and education for the benefit of her empire and her subjects.

There are legions of anecdotes about her personal warmth and

A Baroque oil portrait of Maria Theresia with eleven of her children and her husband, Francis Stephan of Lorraine.

humanity or political vision and acumen, and her reign marks the beginning of a period of transition in how the Habsburgs ruled and perceived themselves. After Maria Theresia, they were not just divinely anointed emperors but also paternalistic public administrators. As rulers, they had subjects, but as bureaucrats, they had to administer an increasingly complex conglomeration of nations.

Political and economic change took place at a slower pace in the Habsburg Empire than in western Europe. The Habsburg Empire was shaken by the shock waves of the French Revolution in 1789 – one of Maria Theresia's daughters, Marie Antoinette, died on the guillotine along with her husband, Louis XVI – and Napoleon invaded the empire a number of times, but the consequences of this period of revolutionary change, as well as the Industrial Revolution which followed shortly thereafter, did not radically transform Austria. On the contrary, after the defeat of Napoleon and the Vienna Congress in

1815, the Habsburg Empire became a bastion of absolutism which successfully suppressed the revolutionary democratic ideals of freedom, liberty, equality and fraternity for well over three decades, and it played an indispensable role in the continental balance of power by holding a key position between the growing Prussian Empire in the Northwest, the Russian Empire in the East, and the deteriorating Turkish Empire of the Balkan Peninsula. The Habsburg Empire lagged behind Western European political and economic developments to such an extent that Karl Marx once epitomized its despotic backwardness by calling it "that European China." (Nowadays critics are not so harsh. Austria is not oriental, it is just Balkan.)

In 1848, revolutions shook many European states along with their absolutistic orders. As a concession to the liberal and nationalistic demands of his subjects, the Austrian Emperor Ferdinand I abdictated to allow his nephew Francis Joseph assume the throne at the age of eighteen. People hoped that Francis Joseph's youth would make him more open to progressive ideas than his predecessors, but in the following sixty-eight years of his reign he showed little sympathy for either liberalism or nationalism, two of the most important 19th century ideologies. Francis Joseph was no friend of innovation in an age of change, and his conservativism is legendary. He hesitated to have modern conveniences like electricity, running water, and flush toilets installed in his residences, and he viewed his subjects' aspirations to democracy with the same suspicion he showed technological progress.

An abbreviated version of Francis Joseph's title shows how diverse the Habsburg holdings had become: "Emperor of Austria, Apostolic King of Hungary, King of Bohemia, of Dalmatia, Croatia, Slavonia, Galicia, Lodomeria, and Illyria,... Archduke of Austria, Grandduke of Tuscany and Cracow, Duke of Lorraine, of Salzburg, Styria, Carinthia, Carniola and Bukovina, Grand Prince of Transylvania, Markgrave of Moravia, Duke of Upper and Lower Silesia, of Modena, Parma,... Count of Habsburg and Tyrol, Count of Feldkirch, Bregenz, Sonnenberg,... Lord of Trieste,... Grand Wojod of Serbia, etc."

This conglomeration of titles shows that the Habsburg Empire was not a modern nation-state. It was an empire full of different nations, each of which had an allegiance to the emperor, who held the whole thing together with a centralized bureaucracy and a multinational army.

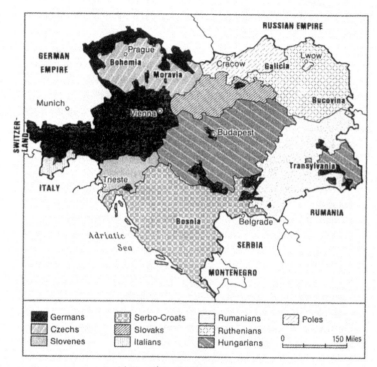

Nationalities in Austria-Hungary.

Francis Joseph also was not a modern politician. He was more of a persistent ruler than an ingenious leader, and he attended to the affairs of state with the diligence of a dedicated civil servant instead of with the flair of a born politician. Even though he considered himself divinely appointed to his position, he also viewed himself as the empire's leading civil servant. He seldom indulged in regal excesses. Being emperor was his job.

It would be incorrect to call all of the territories that Francis Joseph ruled "Austrian" in the modern sense of the word. The German speakers in this empire of some fifty million were a minority – about 20% – while the rest of the population consisted of Czechs, Slovaks, Poles, Ruthenes, Hungarians, Rumanians, Serbs, Croats, Slovenes, and Italians. In an attempt to placate demands made by the Hungarians, the strongest minority, for more national autonomy, the

Habsburg Empire was divided into two semi-autonomous political halves in 1867. The so-called "Compromise" of 1867 created the Dual Monarchy of Austria-Hungary. Francis Joseph was the regent for both halves of the empire, the Emperor of Austria and the King of Hungary. Each half of the monarchy had its own domestic parliament – one in Vienna and one in Budapest – with limited powers. Common concerns such as defense, foreign relations, and financing these joint interests were centrally administered from Vienna, and the Leitha River assumed its old historical role under new political conditions by becoming part of the border between the Austrian and Hungarian halves of the empire. In spite of these reforms, Austria still was a large and multinational concept. The Austrian half of the empire included contemporary Austria, Bohemia and Moravia, southern Poland, parts of the Ukraine, and parts of northern Yugoslavia and Italy, and the Hungarian half covered the rest.

It took the Habsburg dynasty four centuries to build an empire which it lost in the course of four years during World War I. Only in the process of the empire's deterioration did "German-speaking" become synonymous with "Austrian" in our modern and narrow understanding of the term. The small republic which emerged from the shambles of the multinational empire in November 1918 was initially called German-Austria and was merely an amputated version of some of the Habsburgs' oldest holdings. No one was really quite sure what Austria's new role was to be, the Austrians themselves least of all. Geographically, Austria was still the heart of Europe, but politically many Austrians felt that they were in the middle of nowhere.

2. The Imperial Heritage

Austria is often almost exclusively associated with its imperial past or frequently confused with Germany. Germany began to play a much more important role in Europe at about the same time that Austria gradually lost influence in European affairs towards the end of the 19th century. With the collapse of the Habsburg Empire in 1918, Austria assumed a role in Europe comparable to its radically reduced size, and this is one explanation for the fact that so many Austrian associations tend to predate World War I. They have the faded charm of old photographs and awaken nostalgic or sentimental feelings about the good old imperial days of Strauss waltzes, operetta, or the grandfatherly Emperor Francis Joseph. Associations with Germany, on the other hand, are frequently as harsh as a 20th century newsreel: World War I, Hitler (incidentally one of the most frequently disclaimed Austrians), World War II, the Iron Curtain, or the Berlin Wall. However, if these historical associations are not present in one way or the other, Austria is nowadays sometime confused with Germany or demoted to the status of being some kind of a German province.

Austrian and German Empires

Up until 1806, the Habsburgs were the Emperors of the Holy Roman Empire of the German Nation. Satirists never failed to point out that this empire was not holy, not Roman, and for that matter, not an empire. Founded by Charlemagne in the 9th century, it ceased to be a functioning territorial concept in the course of the Middle Ages, but it continued to exist as a cherished fiction for centuries, more a matter of historical prestige than political reality. However, in the course of his various wars with the old European order at the turn of the 19th century, Napoleon forced the Habsburgs to renounce their claim to the title of Holy Roman Emperor which sealed the grave of

Nostalgic imperial associations: a detail from a painting, "Court Ball," by Werner Gause, 1900. Waltzing couples (left) and Emperor Francis Joseph as the center of attention (right).

what retrospectively came to be called the First *Reich* (Empire). The Second and the Third Reich were to follow.

Just before renouncing his old imperial title, Francis II created a new imperial title for himself and his successors: the Emperor of Austria. The Habsburgs were still by far the most powerful German rulers in Europe, Germany being more of a territorial than a political concept at that time. At the beginning of the 19th century, Germany consisted of some thirty-eight more or less independent states of varying size, which were ruled by an array of kings, princes, dukes and counts and included some independent cities. It was not until the second half of the 19th century that Germany became a major European power.

A series of wars and Bismarck's sly foreign policy led gradually to the unification of Germany under the leadership of the Prussians. This enterprise inevitably led to a conflict with the Habsburgs, who took sides against the Prussians in their quest for territorial and political hegemony in Germany.

A war ensued, and the Prussians and their allies decisively defeated the Habsburgs at the Battle of Königgrätz (Sadowa in northern Czechoslovakia) in 1866. For contemporaries, the success of the Prussians was an ominous if not disastrous event. The Habsburgs, pillars of the European order, had been defeated by the Prussians, political upstarts. Königgrätz was the birthplace of the myth of "German superiority," and in Austria today, it is still idiomatically used the same way Waterloo is in English, which clearly indicates the dimensions of the defeat. Johann Strauss composed his famous waltz *On the Blue Danube* shortly after Königgrätz, but it hardly made a dent in the morose atmosphere.

There is also a certain amount of irony in the reasons for the Habsburgs' defeat. The Prussians' military prowess and success were related to the fact that they had equipped their army with modern breech-loading rifles. The inventor of this system had offered his technological achievement to the Austrians decades earlier, but the officials responsible for equipping the Habsburg army failed to recognize its importance. Either old-fashioned or thrifty, they thought it would result in a wasteful use of ammunition and clung to the cumbersome old muzzle-loaded rifles with their ramrods and powderhorns. As a result, Austrian casualties outnumbered the Prussians' six to one.

After Königgrätz, the Prussians proceeded to unify Germany under their leadership, soundly trounced the French in the Franco-Prussian war of 1870, and proclaimed the Second German Reich shortly thereafter. In the decade that followed, the German and the Austrian emperors managed to resolve their differences and became, as Germans natural allies of sorts. However, from this point on, the Habsburgs became more or less junior partners in the sphere of German politics and turned their attention to the Balkan Peninsula, the only avenue left to them for possible political expansion.

The Austrian Idea

Like other foreign threats in the past — the Turks in the 16th and 17th centuries or the Napoleonic invasions around the turn of the 19th century — Austria's war with Prussia evoked a wave of patriotic feeling throughout the Habsburg Empire, but this sentiment should not be confused with nationalism in the modern sense of the word. Within the Habsburgs' multinational empire, patriotism was *Kaisertreue*, allegiance to the emperor; the most famous and frequently uttered oath was *Für Gott, Kaiser und Vaterland*, "for God, the Emperor, and the Fatherland." *Kaiser* was the central concept in this oath because he was Emperor by the Grace of God and His representative on earth, on the one hand, and the patriarch of the various nations and territories of the monarchy, on the other. His imperial decrees began with the phrase: "To My Peoples..."

The fate of the Habsburgs' subjects was inextricably bound with the success and well-being of their rulers, and the idea of *Kaisertreue* reflected a centuries-old union between the rulers and the ruled that transcended local or regional interests. Cultivated predominantly by members of the imperial bureaucracy , the higher echelons of the military, parts of the aristocracy, Roman Catholic clergy, and the conservative members of the bourgeoisie, allegiance to the emperor was not merely the result of centuries of imperial subjugation. It was multinational, even supra-national in spirit. The emperor and his servants stood above the various nationalities and their isolated interests; in serving the parts, they never lost sight of the whole.

This multinational idea allowed the various nationalities of the empire to be Austrian, in the broad sense of the word, without becoming German. After 1918, the term *Alt-Österreicher*, "Old-Austrian," was coined for those "Austrians," who as Germans, Italians, Czechs, Poles, Yugoslavs, or Hungarians, either recognized the former multinational empire as their intellectual and spiritual home or were products of that environment.

Perhaps sensing the impending chaos, the famous Austrian poet and author Hugo von Hofmannsthal wrote a short essay titled *The Austrian Idea* in 1915. Emphasizing "the venerable age of this monarchy and its commanding position in the Southeast on the banks of the largest river which connects Europe with the Orient," Hofmannsthal outlined the Austrian idea in terms of its mission of reconciling "the old European Latin-Germanic with the new Euro-

37

Imperial and Alpine: Emperor Francis Joseph dressed as a hunter, 1910. Hunting was his favorite, practically sole past-time.

pean Slavic world": "The essence of this idea, which has enabled it not only to endure for centuries but also to emerge repeatedly from the chaos and cataclysms of history with a rejuvinated expression, lies in its inner polarity, the antithesis which it encompasses: a borderland, a border wall, the edge of the European empire outside whose gates stretches a chaotically agitated mixture of peoples, half European, half Asian, and, at the same time, a fluid border, a starting point for colonization, for penetration, for the waves of culture that rolled to the East, but also receptive and prepared to receive the westward rolling counterwaves.... The intellectual and spiritual amplitude of this idea surpasses everything the national or economic ideologies of our day can produce."

Lamenting the "liquidation of old supra-national European politics" which had been caused by the rise of national and ideological narrow-mindedness in the second half of the 19th century, Hofmannsthal thought that the Austrian idea, an expression of European culture at its best, could provide the basis for "new supra-national European politics which would fully grasp and integrate the nationality problem," and concluded: "This Europe, which wants to reform itself, needs an Austria." By 1918 most Europeans — with the exception of the Germans in Austria — felt differently.

Universality and reconciliation, not particularity and conflict, were at the heart of Hofmannsthal's definition of the Austrian idea. It is no mere coincidence that Esperanto, the artificial international language invented by the Pole Ludwik Zamenhof in 1887, was very popular in the Habsburg Empire, or that Richard von Coudenhove-Kalergi, the founder of the Pan-European Movement, a post-World War I attempt to revive the Austrian idea on a grand scale, was an Austrian. (It was a source of embarrassment to some people that Franz Jonas, president of Austria from 1965 to 1973, spoke Esperanto; a gentleman by the name of Otto von Habsburg also happens to be one of the leading representatives of the Pan-European Movement today.)

Hofmannsthal obviously overestimated Austria's ability to overcome what he called its "inner polarity," something he idealized as a source of creative energy instead of destructive potential. Another Austrian author, Robert Musil, described Austrian polarities in his novel, *The Man without Qualities,* in terms of the ideological and national conflicts which led to the destruction of the monarchy: "By its constitution it [Austria] was liberal, but its system of government was clerical. The system of government was clerical, but the general attitude to life was liberal. Before the law all citizens were equal, but not everyone, of course, was a citizen. There was a parliament, which made such vigorous use of its liberty that it was usually kept shut; but there was also an emergency powers act by means of which it was possible to manage without Parliament, and every time when everyone was just beginning to rejoice in absolutism, the Crown decreed that there must now again be a return to parliamentary government. Many such things happened in this State, and among them were those national struggles that aroused Europe's curiosity and are today completely misrepresented. They were so violent that several times a year they caused the machinery of State to jam and come to a dead stop. But between times, in the breathing-spaces between government and government, everyone got on excellently with everyone else and behaved as though nothing had ever been the matter." For Musil, the reconciliation of differences in Austria was not a matter of good intentions or supra-national idealism but the paradoxical consequence of ambivalence and inconsistency. One of Francis Joseph's most durable ministers described the strategy for governing under these circumstances as *Weiterwursteln*, "bumbling along."

Nationalism versus Multinationalism

In many respects, the Germans of the Habsburg Empire spoiled the Austrian idea. German-Austrians historically had played a leading role in the multi-national empire and viewed themselves as natural leaders or, in some cases, even as representatives of a superior culture who had helped bring the benefits of German culture to less civilized nations. Initially not such a problem, the relationship of the Germans to the other nationalities of the empire became more and more problematic in the second half of the 19th century. Indeed, one of the long-term and most damaging consequences of the Battle of Königgrätz was that it shook the faith of many German-Austrians, who, in light of the success of Germany, began to view Austria as an anachronism in the age of the modern nation-state. Reinforced by a common language and cultural heritage, more and more German-Austrians, students and members of the upper-middle class in particular, viewed the German Reich with respect or even open admiration. Austria was too old-fashioned, backward, and conservative. This kind of German nationalism helped undermine Austrian multi-nationalism, and in extreme cases it was colored with openly anti-Habsburg, anti-Catholic, and anti-Slav sentiments.

The rise of nationalism among the various peoples of the empire also did its fair share of damage. In 1867, the "Compromise" with Hungary divided the empire into Austrian and Hungarian halves. This idea of "dualism" was seen as a solution to the nationalities problem, since the Hungarians were the strongest and most vocal national group challenging German-Austrians at that time, but it merely split the nationalities problem in two. The German-Austrians had their "domestic" problems with national minorities and the Hungarians had theirs. In many respects, the existence of these two semi-autonomous halves of the empire with different minorities and different policies — combined with the conservativism and longevity of Emperor Francis Joseph — effectively precluded a pluralistic or federalistic solution to the nationalities problem.

In addition to this, the *Reichsrat* (Parliament) for the Austrian half of the monarchy had adopted a constitution with an article which guaranteed equality to each national group. However, nationalistic German-Austrians persistently blocked the realization of this constitutional right to equality because for them it appeared to involve sacrificing their historical "rights" as the leading nation in the multinational empire. One brief example suffices to show how deep national feelings ran.

In 1898 a governmental decree was issued proclaiming that Czech — next to German — was to be recognized as an equal and official language in all public offices of Bohemia and Moravia. All civil servants in those provinces were to learn both languages within the next three years. That Czechs should be able to speak their mother tongue at public offices was by no means an unreasonable request, and since German was the only official language, all of the Czech civil servants knew it anyhow. However, from the German nationalistic point of view, this decree meant German civil servants in those provinces would have to learn Czech, something they regarded as insulting and outrageous. For the German nationalists, the danger of a "Slavification" of the empire appeared imminent, and they managed to block the implementation of the decree by causing a governmental crisis, which resulted in deeper feelings of resentment and more pronounced nationalism on all sides.

The German nationalists' fears of "Slavification" were exaggerated. Even though the representatives from the various Slavic nations held the majority of seats in Austria's multinational parliament, the ideological differences within each national delegation as well as the prejudices among the different nations prevented the formation of any unified Slavic front. The motto Franz Joseph adopted upon assuming the throne was *viribus unitis,* "with united forces," but some historians maintain that Caesar's *divide et impera,* "divide and conquer," would have been more appropriate.

Many representatives of the disadvantaged national minorities called the Habsburg Empire the *Völkerkerker,* "the prison of nations," and they were truly relieved when its collapse allowed them to form their own national states in 1918. However, since 1945 the idea of Old-Austrian or Central European culture has become increasingly popular among the nations that were once part of the monarchy, and it serves as a means of bridging older national differences and newer ideological barriers. These old affinities, of course, occasionally produce unusual results. For example, at the peak of the Solidarity movement in Poland in 1980, a group of elderly citizens from Cracow, which had been the capital of the Habsburg province in southern Poland called Galicia, formed a committee which sought to erect a monument to Emperor Francis Joseph.

Imperially Austrian but Not Really Viennese

A discussion of the Austrian idea need not be confined to the realm of politics. For example, what do most people automatically associate with Austrian cooking? *Wiener Schnitzel* and *Apfelstrudel,* two specialties to which the Viennese have made an almost exclusive claim. To say that Viennese food is the best example of Austrian cuisine inevitably upsets cooks in the provinces of contemporary Austria, who are quick to point out that their own regional recipes and traditions, although not nearly as well known, are just as good and just as Austrian as anything the Viennese can put on the table. The Tyroleans have their *Speckknödel,* a dumpling with bacon stuffing, just as the Viennese have their Schnitzel. In terms of gastronomic citizenship, both are equally Austrian. (Some more examples of this kind of gastronomic diversity are mentioned in the appendix "Typically Provincial.")

Viennese specialties, however, are better examples of Old-Austrian or imperial cooking. Many of the individual recipes so frequently associated with Vienna were not originally Viennese, but became Viennese, and hence Austrian, through a process of assimilation. As the imperial capital and residence, Vienna was not only multinationally but also internationally important. The German author of *The Complete Dictionary of Cooking and Cellars,* a forerunner of today's gastronomic guides which appeared in Hamburg

A detail from a 17th century engraving of an imperial banquet.

in 1716, described the culinary consequences of Vienna's political importance in the following manner: "At the imperial court itself, Spanish, German, French and Hungarian cooking arts are equally concentrated.... I am not wrong when I say that you may meet the best cooks in the world in Austria, the reason being the imperial court and the many foreign princes and ambassadors staying there, who, for the most part, have their own cooks with them, who, in turn, compete with each other to put the best foods on the table. One cook sees, learns, and experiences from the other. The German from the Italian, the Frenchman from the Englishman, and thereafter the common woman assumes some of the practices."

This not only is a description of "international cuisine" at its earliest stages but also shows how foreign foods found their way to the tables of the Viennese. The imperial court adopted the exquisite and the exotic, which was then imitated and simplified by the lower echelons of society. By the time a recipe had filtered down to the common housewife, it was so peculiarly Viennese that no one would consider it foreign. The famous Wiener Schnitzel is a perfect example of this process; it was Italian and imperial before it became Viennese.

The genuine Wiener Schnitzel is merely an imitation of the *costoletta alla milanese*, a breaded veal cutlet named after Milan, the capital of the upper Italian province of Lombardy. The man allegedly responsible for bringing the "Milanese cutlet" to the kitchens of the imperial court was Field Marshal Joseph Radetzky, who, in the process of putting down an uprising against the Habsburgs in Lombardy in 1848, familiarized himself with the local cuisine. After discovering the recipe, he found it delicious enough to pass on to his imperial commanders.

The Wiener Schnitzel is also a good example of how current associations often do not correspond to historical facts. In Vienna today, the common Wiener Schnitzel is made out of pork instead of veal, a sign of its adaption to a normal family budget. Old cookbooks reveal that the Wiener Schnitzel was not popularly called by that name until after 1918, nor were the Viennese frequent Schnitzel-eaters before then. The cattle herds of the nearby Hungarian Plain made beef the cheapest and most frequently served meat in Vienna, but the Viennese seldom roasted or fried it. On the contrary, boiling beef reached the state of a higher art and had the residual benefit of providing a soup before dinner as well.

It was a well-known fact throughout the empire that the favorite meal of Emperor Francis Joseph, a monarch who was legendary for his simple tastes, was boiled beef. (In his case, the beef was a prime cut from the imperial kitchens called *Tafelspitz*, which was so tender it could be cut with a fork.) Mothers throughout Central Europe, who prepared the not-so-prime cuts of beef, never failed to point this out to their children, especially if they were serving fatty pieces or leftovers: "If it is good enough for the Emperor ...."

The Viennese coffee-house, a flourishing institution, at the beginning of the 19th century.

As a matter of fact, meat was scarce in many Austrian households until the middle of the 20th century. An average family had it once a week, usually Sundays, if at all. This scarcity reflects the former low standard of living for broad sections of the population, and it puts those famous and filling Viennese desserts, called *Mehlspeisen* (literally "flour-foods"), in a different light. In most households during the week, a "dessert" like Apfelstrudel was a meal in itself.

Apfelstrudel is another good example of Austrian assimilation. Contrary to many foreign assumptions, the most important part of an Apfelstrudel is not the filling but the dough. A strudel can be filled with other fruits, nuts, cream, cabbage, mushrooms, or meat as well; however, the sign of real quality strudel is the flaky consistency and thinness of the dough, which is not rolled out with a pin but carefully drawn out by hand. (One rule of thumb is that you should be able to

45

read a newspaper through it.) The use of this thin dough is Arabic in origin. The Turks transmitted it to the Hungarians before it made its way to Austria sometime in the late 18th century.

The coffee bean had taken the same route some 100 years earlier which illustrates to what extent the Austrian process of assimilation was not always based on peaceful exchange. In the course of trying to destroy Austrian Christianity, the Turks contributed to the establishment of a quintessentially Viennese institution, the coffeehouse, and what world a piece of strudel be like without its historical predecessor, a cup of coffee?

The best cooks in Vienna during the 19th century provide one last example of successful integration. They were, like the great majority of the city's small tradesmen, craftsmen, and house personnel, Czech immigrants who had come from Bohemia to the big city, and they brought their own recipes along with them. Sweet innovations like *Marillenknödel* (apricot stuffed dumplings made out of potato dough, sprinkled with bread crumbs browned in butter, then served with powdered sugar), took the reverse route of the Wiener Schnitzel. Introduced by lowly immigrants, they gradually made their way up to the tables of the imperial court.

Many Austrian foods and drinks have historical, national, and social genealogies similar to the ones mentioned here. They embody the multinationality of the empire and reflect one of the most positive Old-Austrian traits: the ability to accept and adopt foreign influences by reconciling them with existing traditions.

Austrian cooking is of course still subject to international influences, which sometimes are locally misunderstood. Tourists should be suspicious if they see anything on a menu with the word "Hawaii" next to it. This is usually a traditionally prepared Austrian dish with a slice of canned pineapple on it. Some young Austrian chefs have been infected by French ideas, and they have attempted to create a *nouvelle cuisine autrichienne* with some unusual results. Kiwi is not a good garnish for a Wiener Schnitzel, nor does it taste good in a strudel. Austrian cooking is traditional at best and best when it is prepared traditionally.

Adopted Austrians

A detailed genealogical study of some of Austria's most aristocratic clans or a cursory glance at the Viennese phone book today
document equally well what it once meant to become Austrian.
Among the most blue-blooded Austrian families are the Schwarzen-
bergs, Germans in the Old-Austrian sense of the word; the Hungarian Esterházys; the Czech Kinskys or Lobkowitzs; the Thurn und
Taxis family, German in the German sense of the word; or the Italian
Pallavicinis, just to mention a few. Their lowly-born counterparts have
less striking but equally telling names: Kovacs, Dvorak, Schmidt, or
Rossi. Intermarriage on all levels of society, although seldom across
clearly defined lines of social standing and status, was common in the
old empire, especially in the lowlands and urban centers. Therefore,
the average lowland Austrian in the East is some kind of German-
Czech-Hungarian hybrid, which may be accented by some other
Central European ancestor somewhere along the line. The frequency of "exotic" Central European names drops from East to West
in Austria as the Alps, a natural barrier to assimilation in some
respects, get higher. You do not find too many Dvoraks in Innsbruck;
there is a smattering of Italian names instead, a reminder that the valleys of South Tyrol open up into northern Italy. Along the Carinthian
and Styrian borders the frequency of Slovene names increases, too.

However, being overly sentimental about the Austrian process of
assimilation distorts the historical facts. Different degrees of multinational tolerance existed among the different nations as well as at different social levels. The relationship of Austrians to Hungarians was
frequently characterized by feelings ranging from mild suspicion to
open hostility. Some Austrians, Hungarians, and Czechs had a certain tendency to view the peoples on the Balkan as well as Slovaks as
inferior – with Italians and Poles assuming a status somewhere in between. In Vienna, for example, an aristocrat who spoke German with
a foreign accent may have been regarded as charming, but the
Czech cook who did the same merely betrayed her humble origins.
As a result, many immigrants never taught their own children their
mother tongue. The pressure to assimilate was simply too great.

Some of the most famous examples of Austrian assimilation
come from fields related to imperial service and the arts. The Habsburgs had a long tradition of choosing their aides and advisors on
the basis of merit instead of blood. Among her staff of advisors, for

example, Empress Maria Theresia (1717 — 1780) had Gerhard van Swieten, a Dutch physician who brilliantly advised her on affairs ranging from medicine, higher education, and censorship to church-state relations, and Joseph von Sonnenfels, a professor of law who came from a German rabbinical family, converted to Catholicism, and promoted a broad spectrum of reforms in legal and administrative affairs, the humanization of the penal code and procedures in particular. Both of these men are superb examples of commoners who advanced to the very top of the imperial bureaucracy. Maria Theresia's right-hand man was Prince Wenzel Anton Kaunitz-Rietberg, a Czech-German hybrid, who filled the two most important appointed positions in the empire, court chancellor and state chancellor, from 1753 to 1792. Longevity of service at this high level was matched later only by a German whose policies were synonymous with Austrian politics in the first half of the 19th century: Prince Clemens Lothar von Metternich.

Examples of this sort can be found in all branches and at all levels of imperial service, the army being an illustration of multinationality par excellence. Certainly there were aristocratic cliques at the top of the chain of command, but beneath that level loyalty and performance were the ticket to social mobility. Promotion was based on merit.

The most famous commanders of the imperial armies were Prince Eugene of Savoy, an outstanding soldier of Italian, French, and German origins, who served three Habsburg emperors and was instrumental in defeating the Turks at the end of the 17th century, and Field Marshal Count Joseph Radetzky, a Bohemian-Hungarian hybrid, renowned for his strategic brilliance, dedication, and longevity. Serving in virtually every war the Habsburgs fought from 1784 until 1849, Radetzky died in 1857 at the age of eighty-three, still actively serving as the imperially appointed governor of the northern Italian province of Lombardy-Venetia.

The rank-and-file soldiers of the imperial army also reflected the same multinationality. When World War I broke out, only twenty-five out of every one hundred soldiers in the Habsburgs' army were German; forty-four belonged to the various Slavic nations; twenty-three were Hungarian; and eight were Italian or Rumanian.

In terms of Austrian cultural achievements, the Viennese in particular have a way of turning "foreigners" into native sons. Franz Schubert and the various members of the waltz-composing Strauss

Two famous composers: Johann Strauss, Viennese-born (left), and Johannes Brahms, Viennese by choice, on the veranda of Strauss' villa in Bad Ischl.

dynasty are the only Viennese-born composers from that long list normally associated with the city. Joseph Haydn is claimed by the Austrians and Hungarians alike. Some of his distant ancestors were Hungarian, and one of the leading Hungarian aristocratic families, the Esterházys, were his first patrons. Wolfgang Amadeus Mozart is Salzburg's musical claim to fame. Ludwig van Beethoven and Johannes Brahms were both Germans by birth, Viennese by destiny or choice, and Gustav Mahler came from a Bohemian-Jewish family.

Last of all, it is important to mention those Austrians who were never offically recognized as a national group within the multinational empire but nevertheless provided some of the best representatives of Austrian culture, the Jews. There is an important distinction between Old-Austrian Orthodox Jewish culture and assimilated Jews' contributions to what is commonly referred to as Austrian culture. The best examples of Orthodox Jewish culture were found in Galicia and Bukovina, the crownlands in southern Poland and the western Ukraine which had the largest unassimilated Jewish populations. Only a relatively small group of prosperous, well-educated, upper-middle-class Jews became assimilated in the larger urban centers like Budapest, Vienna, or Prague.

Effectively liberated by the constitutional rights granted all citizens in 1867, some Jews abandoned their orthodox beliefs, migrated from the ghettos of the East to the cities in the West, and embraced secular ideologies which facilitated assimilation: liberalism and later, in many cases, socialism. Excluded by birth from the constraints of aristocratic or Catholic conservativism, they often adopted progressive attitudes or causes ranging from stylistic questions in the arts to politics. Jewish by birth or heritage, they frequently defined and understood themselves primarily as Austrians.

The fact that Theodor Herzl, a Hungarian-Jewish liberal journalist, the author of The Jewish State, and hence the intellectual father of the Zionistic movement and the state of Israel, as well as Adolf Hitler, an unsuccessful artist from the provinces, author of Mein Kampf, and the political father of the Holocaust, were both products of Austrian culture at the turn of the century tends to obscure the status Jews had in Austria. In the Austro-Hungarian Empire, there was a highly differentiated spectrum of attitudes towards Jews as well as among Jews themselves. The virulent racism and anti-semitism which impressed the young Hitler was one extreme, but there was toleration or acceptance of the Jews also. Many Orthodox Jews preferred life in traditional ghetto communities and strongly disapproved of assimilation, and most of Herzl's Jewish contemporaries thought that the idea of a separate Jewish state was incredulous. In between these various extremes, many Jews had found a home in Austria.

Stefan Zweig, an author who was a product of bourgeois-Jewish assimilation, indicated in his autobiography, The World of Yesterday, that Austria's conciliatory nature was the prerequisite for the fortunate and productive relationship Jews had to Austrian and specifically Viennese culture. Since Zweig committed suicide as a heart-broken emigré in Brazil in 1942, this may appear to be a nostalgic glorification. Nevertheless, he emphasized the tolerant atmosphere which prevailed in Austria despite the pointed conflicts within the empire, and he pointed out that Jewish intellectuals and artists found a unique environment in Vienna around the turn of the century that spurred their sensibilities and productivity. Zweig stressed that these Jews were productive "by no means in a specifically Jewish manner, but that they, through a wondrous act of empathy, managed to most intensely express the Viennese, the Austrian spirit (Österreichertum)." In other words, assimilated Jewish intellectuals and artists, who rejected the ideas of confessional and national particularism, embodied the Austrian idea and captured best the brilliance and darkness of imperial Austria in their works. What would the Austrian contribution to the 20th century look like without Austrians like Mahler and Schönberg, Kafka and Hofmannsthal, or Wittgenstein and Freud?

3. Killing the Heir and the Empire

On the morning of June 28, 1914, a motorcade of six cars drove down the Apple Quay, the broadest boulevard in Sarajevo, the capital of one of the Habsburgs' most recent acquisitions, Bosnia. The street was lined with spectators waiting to see Archduke Francis Ferdinand, the nephew and designated heir of Emperor Francis Joseph. Along the way, a bystander threw a small black object at the archduke's open car. It grazed his wife's neck, bounced onto the convertible's trunk, then fell down onto the street where it exploded, injuring two men in the following vehicle. In spite of the archduke's importance, security measures surrounding his visit were unusually lax.

Arriving at city hall, the archduke and the mayor of Sarajevo made a strained attempt to conduct their trivial exchange of courtesies calmly. Fearing another attempt on the archduke's life, one of his aides suggested that troops be brought in to clear the streets. The military governor of Bosnia dismissed those fears as exaggerated and vetoed the idea with the objection that the troops were not in the dress uniforms protocol demanded for a visitor of the archduke's status.

The officials responsible hastily reorganized Francis Ferdinand's itinerary and the route of his motorcade because the archduke, an impulsive man on occasion, insisted on visiting the injured members of his party who had been taken to a local hospital. Apparently due to a misunderstanding, the lead car in the motorcade made a wrong turn, and the archduke's chauffeur stopped to back up and change his route. Standing on the sidewalk among the people anxiously waiting for a glimpse of the heir to the Emperor of Austria, Gavrilo Princip must have been surprised when the open car carrying Archduke Francis Ferdinand and his wife, Sophie, stopped right in front of him. The nineteen-year-old Serbian nationalist, a member of a terrorist organization called the Black Hand which was dedicated to the unification of all Serbs in one state, stepped out of the crowd and drew his pistol. Standing about five feet away from the archduke's

The assassination of Archduke Francis Ferdinand and his wife on June 28, 1914 in Sarajevo; a drawing by Felix Schwormstädt.

car, Princip fired two shots. The first of his bullets hit Sophie in the abdomen. Princip was not an experienced marksman, his hand was apparently raised by the kick of the first shot; the second bullet hit Francis Ferdinand in the neck. The wounded couple lost consciousness in the course of being rushed to the military governor's mansion. Beyond medical help, they died ten minutes apart from each other shortly before 11 a. m.

The news of Francis Ferdinand's assassination reached Emperor Francis Joseph in Bad Ischl, an Alpine spa in one of the most scenic parts of the province of Upper Austria, the *Salzkammergut*, where the emperor traditionally spent his summer vacation making the town the "center of the empire" for a few weeks. Francis Joseph was personally and politically estranged from his nephew, and the assassination hurt his imperial prestige more than anything else. He immediately returned to Vienna, and one month later signed a declaration of war on Serbia, a small but energetic state of five million which promoted the cause of Pan-Slavism and had harbored the assassins.

Gavrilo Princip and a number of his accomplices were put on trial. Princip was too young to be sentenced to death and began serving a life term in Theresienstadt, an imperial fortress and prison near Prague which later gained an infamous reputation as a Nazi concentration camp. Chained to the wall in a dark cell, he died of tuberculosis after two years. As an act of Slavic solidarity after World War I, Czechoslovakia transferred the remains of Princip, who had since become a national hero, to Yugoslavia, and in Sarajevo a plaque was inset in the street to commemorate the spot where he stood when the shots he fired began the liberation of the Slavic peoples from Habsburg domination. Not to be outdone, Austria has the automobile in which Francis Ferdinand was assassinated as well as his bloodstained uniform on exhibit in Vienna's Museum of Military History.

Starting the Great War

The Balkan Peninsula was a source of trouble throughout the 19th century. The declining Ottoman Empire had gradually lost control over territories and peoples it had ruled for some five hundred years, and this process of deterioration upset the traditional balance of power in southeastern Europe. It gave the peoples of the Balkans an opportunity to free themselves from foreign rule and, at the same time, opened up avenues of expansion for Europe's great powers. Small states like Rumania, Bulgaria, Montenegro, and Serbia fought either with Turkey or among themselves over territorial claims which led from one crisis to the next. At the same time, Italy, Austria-Hungary, Russia, and England all attempted to expand their spheres of influence at the expense of the Turks in the Adriatic, on the Balkan Pensinsula, or in the Mediterranean Sea.

Bosnia and Herzegovina, today parts of south-central Yugoslavia, were the most recent additions to the Habsburg Empire. Occupied and administered as a protectorate since 1878, these provinces were unilaterally annexed by Austria-Hungary in 1908 in violation of several international agreements. Aside from provoking a series of international protests, this action raised the suspicion of the Russian czar, who regarded himself as the protector and promoter of Slavic nations. It also completely alienated the state of Serbia and enraged the population of Bosnia, four-fifths of which was Serbian.

Before the annexation, the Serbs had viewed the Habsburgs at best as benevolent caretakers who had helped liberate Bosnia and Herzegovina from the yoke of Turkish rule. Frequently, however, the Habsburgs were viewed as undesirable and transitory foreign administrators who some day would be forced out by the unification of all Serbs in one state. The unexpected annexation of the contested provinces shattered the dream of Serbian national unity and made the Habsburgs hated symbols of injustice and oppression.

The idea of Southern Slavic unification was a nightmare for the Habsburgs. After all, similar enterprises of national unification initiated by other small states in the past had ended in catastrophes. Piedmont had forced them out of Northern Italy in 1859, and Prussia had ousted them from the realm of German politics altogether in 1866. Before 1914, some Austrian imperial advisors favored the idea of a preventive war with Serbia to take care of things before they got out of hand, but the assassination of Francis Ferdinand provided a perfectly legitimate reason to settle scores with Serbia, which was seen as a small and insolent troublemaker.

There is a certain amount of irony in the fact that Francis Ferdinand was a victim of Slavic nationalism. A progressive thinker, he had expressed great reservations about the annexation of the Slavic territories in the first place and was a proponent of reorganizing the empire in a manner which would have granted its various national groups more autonomy. This was exactly the kind of thinking for which his eighty-four-year-old uncle, Francis Joseph, showed little understanding, nor did it interest most Serbs, whose goal was national unification, not more lenient subjugation.

The Austro-Hungarian conflict with Serbia could have remained a mere regional one if it had not been for a generous amount of chauvinism and diplomatic bungling on all sides, combined with a fatal network of treaties. The murder of Francis Ferdinand was not one of the deep-seated causes of World War I, but it provided an occasion for it to begin.

By 1914, the major European powers had aligned themselves into two defensive blocs. A German-Austro-Hungarian alliance from 1878 provided the backbone for one military configuration which was initially directed against the possibility of Russian aggression. Italy joined this complex in 1882, essentially seeking German support in the event of a war instigated by France, which completed the Triple Alliance. (The Austro-Hungarian partnership with Italy was highly artificial because they were traditional enemies with conflicting interests in northern Italy as well as in the Adriatic.)

Fearing isolation, France and Russia formed an alliance in 1893 which provided the basis for a second network of treaties. Russia was concerned about the prospects of German and Austro-Hungarian aggression, and France was interested in insuring itself against the eventuality of a joint German-Italian attack. By 1907, England had reached "cordial understandings" with France and Russia, her traditional enemies, and these agreements completed the Triple Entente.

It is important to stress the fact that both of these alliance systems were defensive in character. In those days, they were viewed as a means of preventing a direct conflict among major European powers. However, one thing they did not take into account was the possibility of a peripheral, regional conflict — like the Austro-Hungarian-Serbian one on the Balkan Peninsula — turning into a full-fledged European war. This is exactly what political recklessness produced; Austria-Hungary and Serbia, Germany and Russia, all gambled in 1914 and lost.

Germany, for example, was by no means committed to support Austria-Hungary in its war against Serbia, but Austria-Hungary asked for and categorically received German support. Russia, on the other hand, was not contractually obligated to support Serbia, but it viewed itself as the protector of all Slavs and was not going to tolerate any bullying. The Austro-Hungarian ultimatum delivered to the Serbs three weeks after the assassination was formulated in terms which were so unacceptable that they had to be rejected, and the Serbs did just that after securing Russian support. Two days after the Austro-Hungarian declaration of war on Serbia, the czar ordered the Russian army to mobilize, and the German emperor, in turn, demanded that the mobilization order be retracted. The czar's refusal to do so led to the German-Austro-Hungarian declaration of war on Russia. This turn of events pulled France, which had no intention of fighting a war for Serbia, into the whole affair and started a fatal chain reaction.

Nevertheless, the outbreak of the war evoked waves of patriotic enthusiasm throughout Europe. Everyone thought in terms of a quick victory; no one anticipated four years of trench warfare or the consequences of murderous innovations like the machine gun or poisonous gas. The German-Austro-Hungarian plan for winning the war was based on a relatively simple one-two punch strategy. The Germans had planned on quickly defeating the French before the British could land enough expeditionary forces to make a decisive difference. The Austrians intended to dispatch easily with the hopelessly outnumbered Serbs and then hold the eastern front which, due to the anticipated slowness of the Russian mobilization, should have been no great problem. Expecting quick initial victories, the German and Austro-Hungarian armies subsequently were supposed to unite their forces in the East in order to defeat Russia.

As things turned out, neither the German nor the Austro-Hungarian armies achieved their immediate objectives of quickly knocking their direct opponents out of the war, and the Russian army mobilized much more quickly than expected. These miscalculations resulted in demoralizing and costly losses in the East at the beginning of the war and produced the worst of all strategic scenarios: a protracted war on two fronts with a division of forces that would not allow a decisive victory on either.

Ending the Empire

World War I most frequently evokes associations of trench warfare on the western front, the bloody battles of attrition between the Germans and the French. Austro-Hungarian armies were engaged in three less well-known but equally dramatic theaters of war: in the East, on the Balkan Peninsula, and in northern Italy. By the end of 1916, Austria-Hungary had more or less achieved its military objectives. In the East, the Russians had been forced into the defensive, where they were to remain for the rest of the war. The Austro-Hun-

War in the mountains on the Italian front: Austrian soldiers positioned above crosses marking graves.

garian army had occupied Serbia as well as Rumania, which had entered the war on the side of the Entente powers in 1916 in hopes of making territorial gains at the expense of the Habsburg Empire. Italy had declared war on Austria-Hungary in 1915 after signing the secret Treaty of London with the Entente powers which promised major territorial concessions in Tyrol and the Northern Adriatic in exchange for Italy's participation, but the Italian front was as stable as its French counterpart. From 1915 until 1917, a series of eleven major battles along the Isonzo River (near today's Italian-Yugoslav border) resulted in tremendous losses and negligible gains for both sides.

The fact that Italy and Rumania entered the war against the Habsburgs actually provoked indignation throughout the empire and raised multinational morale; it was clear who the enemies were:

traitors like Italy and Rumania, murderers like the Serbs, and the czar, a despot and imperialist. It would be an exaggeration to call the war popular, but in spite of the losses and hardships, it rallied sympathies for the Habsburgs' cause and the Austrian idea. There were, for example, some Slavic soldiers who deserted from the Habsburg armies, but this was an exception, by no means the rule. Like other foreign threats in the past, the war initially promoted more loyalty and supra-national patriotism than nationalistic discontent.

One of Austria-Hungary's biggest problems was its closest ally. On the one hand, Germany and Austria-Hungary were bound to each other by a treaty that was morally reinforced by the military honor code of comrades-in-arms, but, on the other, Austria-Hungary's strategic and political interests were completely different from those of Germany. The exaggerated respect many leading Austrians showed for Germany made them either unwilling or unable to assert themselves in the best interests of Austria which, as time passed, became more and more subordinated to the German goal of winning a war that could not be won. Treated by Germany with a mixture of scepticism and condescension, Austria-Hungary gradually acquiesced to the role of junior partner in the alliance.

In 1917, two events changed the entire complexion of the war: the German declaration of unlimited submarine warfare, a measure which the Austrians opposed but did not block, and the Russian Revolution. The former brought the United States into the war and provided the Entente powers with a gigantic, fresh reservoir of men and materials which proved to be decisive; the latter eventually knocked the Russians out of the war, which freed German and Austro-Hungarian troops to be transferred to the French and Italian fronts. However, their presence there, in spite of high expectations to the contrary, did not affect the ultimate course of events.

The Russian Revolution and the United States' engagement also shifted the ideological perspective of the war. The czar, undoubtedly the most despotic ruler in Europe, disappeared as an Entente ally, which had the propagandistic side effect of making Germany and Austria Europe's sole representatives of "tyranny." Now the Entente powers and the USA were fighting for freedom and democracy in Central Europe and against the imperialistic aspirations of the German emperor as well as against the subjugation of various nationalities by the Habsburgs.

The death of Emperor Francis Joseph in November 1916 was a

warning of things to come. The passing away of the eighty-six-year-old patriarch, who had ruled twelve nations for three generations, symbolically marked the end of an era, a way of life, perhaps even a world-view. Nothing was really the same after the "old Kaiser" was gone.

Francis Joseph left his twenty-nine-year-old successor and grandnephew, Karl I, with a precarious political inheritance. Emperor Karl realized that he had to get Austria-Hungary out of the war, the hardships of which were becoming a real source of domestic discontent, and simultaneously reorganize the empire to satisfy the various nations' long-standing demands for more autonomy. However, he lacked the daring and experience, as well as the personal strength and political support, necessary to abandon the German alliance or energetically begin solving the nationalities problem. As a result, he lost his only chance for political credibility with the Entente powers and many of his own subjects. International and domestic attitudes towards Austria then evolved in a completely unanticipated direction.

At the beginning of World War I, the Entente powers did not have the slightest intention of dismembering the Habsburg Empire. Certainly territorial concessions would have to be made to allies like Italy and Rumania, and the question of Poland, divided for over a century among the German, Austrian, and Russian empires, had to be resolved. Nevertheless, the Austro-Hungarian Empire was still considered to be an essential element in the continental balance of power. It was not until the very end of the war that this thinking changed drastically under the influence of the American president, Woodrow Wilson.

In January 1918, Wilson outlined his famous political program for post-World War Europe, the "Fourteen Points." Three points directly referred to the Habsburg Empire: the reestablishment of Poland; a readjustment of the borders of Italy "along clearly recognizable lines of nationality;" and the provision that "the peoples of Austria-Hungary ... should be accorded the freest opportunity of autonomous development." At that time, the last, rather vague formulation referred to the necessity for some sort of a domestic reorganization of the Habsburg Empire, but by the time the war drew to an end it had been reinterpreted to mean "national self-determination," the creation of small, independent nation-states at the expense of the empire.

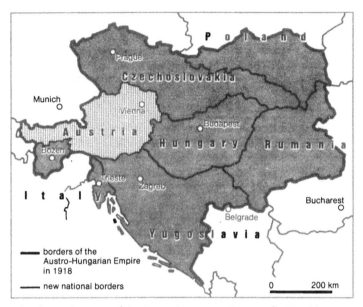

The dismemberment of the Austro-Hungarian Empire after World War I.

This shift in policy reflected a number of different interests and expectations. There were a variety of democratic and nationalistic arguments for the Central European peoples' right to self-determination. One of the most successful crusaders for this cause in the West was Tomas Masaryk, the founding father of the Czechoslovak republic. Formerly a Czech representative to Austria's multinational parliament before the war and an associate professor of philosophy at the University of Vienna, Masaryk knew his Habsburg enemy well. He skillfully organized the support and sympathies of Western politicians and public opinion for the cause of Czechoslovak independence, which coincidentally also paved the way for the creation of Yugoslavia.

The idea of national self-determination was also reinforced by less idealistic political and strategic arguments. The newly founded Central European states were supposed to resolve the nationalities problem and, at the same time, create a buffer of democracy against the possibility of future German aggression. Their creation was to be a guarantee for peace and security in Europe and had the concomitant benefit of destroying Germany's largest and most loyal ally.

During the summer of 1918, German and Austrian resistance on the French and Italian fronts slowly began to deteriorate which was merely the military prelude to an impending political debacle. In mid-October, Emperor Karl issued a manifesto declaring a federal reorganization of the Austrian half of the empire, in which each nation was to have its own state. By that time, however, Czechoslovakia and Yugoslavia were already in the process of being founded, and Karl's manifesto had the side effect of dissolving the partnership with Hungary which also began to go its own way. On October 26, 1918, Karl finally abandoned the alliance with Germany, one week before Austria-Hungary signed a cease-fire agreement with the Entente powers, but these concessions were too little and too late. The empire was already in shambles, and on November 11, 1918, Emperor Karl ended over six centuries of Habsburg rule by officially proclaiming his withdrawal from state affairs.

German-Austria

The imminent collapse of the empire prodded the German-speaking representatives of the parliament for the Austrian half of the monarchy into action. On October 21, 1918, they formed the Provisional National Assembly for German-Austria in an attempt to exercise national self-determination for the Germans in the Habsburg Empire, too. These representatives planned to establish a state encompassing all of the German-speaking territories of the empire, and they expressed their willingness to enter into some kind of confederation with the other democratic states which were in the process of carving themselves out of the empire.

The idea of a confederation of democracies in place of the Habsburg Empire might seem peculiar to the modern observer, but this desire was much more than a conservative scheme for a post-imperial empire. Austria's largest party on the left, the Social Democrats, had a long tradition of working for national equality and autonomy within the framework of the empire, and many socialists rejected the idea of nationalism as bourgeois and reactionary. For them, the "de-imperialization" of Austria was no reason to abandon the Austrian idea. On the contrary, they hoped that it would be possible to rejuvinate the Austrian idea of supra-nationality with the democratic spirit of socialist internationalism. After all, Marx ended the *Communist Manifesto* with the imperative: "Workers of the world unite!" Austrian Social Democrats wanted the oppressed peoples of Central Europe to do just that. Austria's other major party, the conservative Christian Social Party, also supported the confederation idea, but for different ideological and predominantly economic reasons.

The fact that Austrian socialists and conservatives saw eye-to-eye on this issue shows to what extent German-Austrians thought the territorial dismemberment of the Habsburg Empire meant the destruction of a centuries-old community of economic and political interests. The other nationalities, however, viewed the end of the empire not only as a liberation from the Habsburgs but also as the end of centuries of German hegemony. Austria's neighbors consequently rejected offers to confederate which appeared to leave German-speaking politicians with only one other alternative.

On November 12, 1918, the day after Emperor Karl withdrew from state affairs, a provisional government organized by the political parties in conjunction with the National Assembly proclaimed the foundation of the Republic of German-Austria from the ramp of the Parliament in Vienna, and the second article of this proclamation stated that the newly founded republic was part of Germany. Across the entire political spectrum, leading politicans in Austria had been forced to drop their plans for a democratic modification of the Old-Austrian idea and place their hopes in a unification *(Anschluss)* with Germany.

Two problems plagued Austria from the moment of its inception: widespread doubts about its viability and the virtual absence of a national identity. The dismemberment of the Habsburg Empire broke up a largely self-sufficient economic unit into its constituent parts. As a result, Austria's economy was left hopelessly overdeveloped in some sectors, like the metal and finishing industries, and underdeveloped in others, like textile production and agriculture. Before World War I, for example, Vienna's most important rail connections were to the North (Czechoslovakia and Poland) and the East (Hungary).

The economic consequences of Central Europe's new political borders were catastrophic for Austria which lost its traditional suppliers of raw materials and markets for its goods. Previously dependent upon Czech and Polish coal for heating and generating electricity,

The proclamation of the First Republic from the ramp of Parliament in Vienna on November 12, 1918.

Austria could only cover one percent of its needs from domestic sources. Production and public transportation practically came to a standstill. Unemployment skyrocketed as shortages became more and more acute.

The situation in the food sector was critical. Vienna had drawn most of its foodstuffs from Hungary, and the Austrian provinces were neither willing nor able to compensate for the enormous shortages which existed in the city after the war. In 1913, 900,000 liters of milk were delivered to Vienna daily; by 1920, it was 15 times less. The structural problems of the Austrian economy appeared insoluble; under these circumstances, unification with Germany seemed to be the small state's only chance for survival.

Before 1918, the concept of Austrian nationalism would have been a contradiction of terms because Austria was by definition imperially multinational, and within the multinational framework of the empire those people we now call Austrians considered themselves Germans. Therefore, in 1918, Austria was merely a territorial concept for the former German-speaking areas of the empire, and the only kind of existing nationalism there was German.

In addition to these problems, Austrians were accustomed to thinking in grander political dimensions. No one saw of German-Austria's future in terms of a small state like Switzerland or Belgium; leading politicians in Austria embraced the idea of an Anschluss with Germany. For German nationalists, this was a dream come true; for Social Democrats, it meant the unification of the German-speaking proletariat and an opportunity to join forces with their ideological counterparts in Germany, home of one of the largest and strongest working class organizations in Europe; and for the conservative Christian Social movement, it appeared to be the only reasonable political and economic alternative.

Big Loser: Small State

The politicians of the provisional government were also faced with a series of other problems. Public administration and security had effectively collapsed. Elections had to be held and a constitution had to be drafted, but each political party had its own ideas about how the republic should look. Due to conflicting claims with Austria's neighbors, the provisional government also was not sure what the borders of German-Austria were, nor did it know how the new state was going to be treated by the victorious powers. Some of these open questions were answered at the Paris Peace Conference in the summer of 1919.

Dr. Karl Renner, the Social Democratic chancellor of the provisional government, headed the Austrian delegation which met with the representatives of the victorious powers in a suburb of Paris,

Saint-Germain. The Austrian delegation hardly received a welcome worthy of high-ranking diplomats. They resided in a gilded cage – a small palace surrounded by barbed wire – and after their first meeting at the conference one thing became perfectly clear: German-Austria was not a partner in the negotiations, but an object of negotiation among the victorious powers.

The Austrian delegation came prepared to document its case on three vital questions: the importance of the Anschluss, the fact that German-Austria did not consider itself a legal successor to the Habsburg Empire, and Austria's border claims. The victorious powers did not make a major concession on any of these points. Unilaterally changing the name of German-Austria to Austria, they forbade an Anschluss with Germany.

Renner argued eloquently that Austria was not the legal successor to the Habsburg Empire but was a new state like Czechoslovakia. Therefore, reparations, if any, would have to be shared by all the peoples who had fought in the Habsburg's war. Rejecting this interpretation, the victorious powers burdened Austria with reparations, a load which its already unstable economy could barely carry.

Appealing to the principle of national self-determination, the Austrian delegation then argued that all German-speaking territories should be part of the republic. Using its own version of the viability argument, Czechoslovakia claimed the historical borders of Bohemia and Moravia for economic reasons and for the sake of establishing a defensible natural frontier. The conference agreed with the Czechs, and in doing so, created a German-speaking minority of three million inside Czechoslovakia.

Creating the impression that South Tyrol was much more Italian than it really was, Italy pretended that the only way its future national security could be ensured was by moving the Italian border up to the strategically important Brenner Pass. Consequently, the new Austrian-Italian border was not drawn along "clearly recognizable lines of nationality." On the contrary, it partitioned Tyrol, and put 250,000 German-speaking Tyroleans inside Italian frontiers.

The manner in which national self-determination was handled at the Paris Peace Conference merely subdivided and, in some cases, inverted imperial Austria's nationalities problem. In Czechoslovakia and Italy, the former German "oppressors" became minorities, and a similar situation existed for Hungarians in Czechoslovakia and Rumania. Every Central European state had some kind of conflict with its neighbors related to "new" national minorities created by the freshly drawn borders.

The situation on the border between Yugoslavia and Austria was critical. In December 1918, the newly established Kingdom of Yugoslavia began occupying the Carinthian and Styrian borderlands which had traditionally been inhabited by a mixture of German-Austrians and Slovenes in an attempt to realize its national border claims by force. Austria had virtually no army, so the defense of Carinthia and Styria was left up to a hastily organized "peoples army" (*Volkswehr*) which was supported by locally organized "home defense leagues" (*Heimwehr*). One of the peculiarities of this conflict was that some Austrians and Yugoslavs, who had fought side-by-side in the imperial army a few months previously, were now fighting each other.

After six months of bloodshed, this border question was resolved partially at the conference table and partially at the ballot box. Some parts of southern Carinthia and Styria were ceded outright to Yugoslavia, and a plebiscite was held in other parts of southern Carinthia to let the mixed German-speaking and Slovene population decide their own citizenship. They voted for Austria, or at least for Carinthia.

There was sporadic fighting along the Hungarian frontier, too. Hungary demanded territories east of the Leitha River that historically had been part of a province in the Hungarian half of the empire called West-Hungary. Austria, however, claimed regions with predominantly German-speaking populations. Austria and Hungary finally reached a diplomatic compromise through which part of the territory in question was to be ceded to Austria in two phases, but after the first transfer of territory, Hungary decided that it was enough and violated a number of international agreements by keeping the rest. The territory Austria did acquire became the province of Burgenland.

Even though the conditions of the Treaty of Saint-Germain were much worse than the Austrians had anticipated, the treaty was signed and ratified under protest because it was a *fait accompli*. When Renner returned to Vienna with the Austrian delegation, he was met at Vienna's West Train Station by a large crowd and icy silence. One man broke through the police lines, ran up to Renner, and said: "You wimp! They sent such an idiot to Saint-Germain, and he let himself get duped by Clemenceau [the French foreign minister].

Aren't you ashamed of yourself, you country bumpkin. You should've told 'm: 'Kiss my ass.' "

Police apprehended the man quickly, but Renner told them to let him go, asked the man for his name and address, and had his secretary take them down. Turning to the man, Renner said: "You're right. If there is another war and we lose it, we have to send the right representative to Saint-Germain. Then you come along." The man looked baffled at first and then laughed heartily, relaxing the tense atmosphere.

This anecdote not only shows how unhappy the general populace was about the conditions of the Treaty of Saint-Germain. It is also a good example of Renner's poise and his Austrian sense of humor: irony and self-irony in the face of disaster. Austria's situation at that time appeared disastrous indeed.

4. Austrian Polarities

The dismemberment of the Habsburg Empire resolved the polarities of the Old-Austrian idea in a destructive manner, but within the borders of the Austrian republic new ones emerged. Conflicts which had been latent, reconciled, or repressed before 1918, erupted under radically new circumstances and overshadowed the post-imperial and republican idea of Austria. Various kinds of German nationalism, provincial traditionalism, and ideological particularism undermined the republic from the start.

After World War I, a few isolated individuals tried to point out that Austria in fact had a long tradition of unity and viability. After all, the new Austrian republic corresponded roughly to the hereditary lands of the Habsburgs in 1500, or, for that matter, to the old Roman province of *Noricum*. These profound historical arguments impressed very few contemporaries. Unlike the peoples of other Central European states that had carved themselves out of the empire, the Austrians in the German-speaking provinces had no tradition of striving for unity and national independence. On the contrary, they felt stuck with what was left over after all of the other nations of the empire had settled their claims to national self-determination, and for most Austrians national self-determination meant unification with Germany, something the victorious powers had forbidden.

The attitudes of Austria's political parties as well as its individual provinces towards the republic were rather ambivalent. Austrian politicians felt they had to make the best out of a bad situation. The provinces had a tendency to look towards their own regional traditions and historical autonomy as a source of identity, and they initially demonstrated a very low degree of commitment to the republic. In 1918, Austrians generally identified themselves with the fact that they were German first, either a provincial tradition or political party second, and Austria last and least of all.

69

Austrians and Germans

The great common bonds between Austria and Germany were language, culture, and history. After all, Austria could trace its German heritage back over a thousand years and historically had always fulfilled a "German mission" in the East. The Habsburgs had been the emperors of the Holy Roman Empire and played a leading role in German politics right up into the 19th century. Before the unification of Germany, Austrians were one of the many different political subcategories of Germans, like the Bavarians, Saxons, Rhinelanders, or Prussians.

However, the unification of Germany under the Prussians and the proclamation of a new German Reich in 1871 simplified the basis for all future comparisons. The birth of many German and Austrian clichés, which are still in circulation today, was politically inspired. There were *Reichsdeutsche*, literally "Germans from the Reich," with their proverbial efficiency, sense of duty, assertiveness, and firmness of character, and Austrians: *Gemütlichkeit*, understanding, submissiveness, and charm. German culture was Protestant, abstract, and austere; Austrian culture was Catholic, aesthetic, and sensuous.

In spite of the obvious differences in national temperament and sensibility, Austrians identified themselves with the universality of the idea of German culture and saw themselves as belonging to a larger linguistic, cultural, and historical community called the German nation. Austrians sought the ideal or abstract similarities between their own and German traditions instead of the particular and concrete differences. From today's point of view, this may seem a bit difficult to understand because Austrians now fundamentally define themselves in terms of their differences from the Germans; but, after World War I this kind of pro-Austrian attitude was rare and a sign of provincialism. Hardly anyone was prepared to abandon the idea of being German for the sake of being just Austrian.

Due to their historical experience, Austrians also had a profound need to be part of something larger, some kind of post-imperial fixation on grander dimensions. This desire is one possible psychological explanation for the Austrian fascination with the Anschluss (and in some respects also a source of today's nostalgic glorification of the imperial days). It is important to note, however, that the Austrians' relationship to the Germans was rather asymmetrical. Austrians considered themselves more German than the Germans considered them German, and the Anschluss as an objective political goal and as a subjective psychological need enjoyed a much higher priority in Austrian hearts and minds than in German ones. After 1918, Austrians frequently suffered from the feelings of inadequacy or inferiority that go along with being a smaller and weaker sibling. The legal abstraction of Austrian citizenship was not enough to inspire Austrians with a sense of nationalism or patriotism. There was one German nation but two German states, and Austria was literally and figuratively the second one.

Mountain and Valley Mentalities

One of the peculiarities of the Austrian compass is that it has only three points. Austrians speak about their own country in terms of the West, the South, and the East. Vorarlberg, Tyrol, and Salzburg are in the West; Carinthia and Styria are in the South; and Lower Austria, Vienna, and Burgenland are in the East. (The province of Upper Austria is a fence-straddler or an area of transition between East and West.) The fact that northern and eastern Austria are collapsed into one concept, the East, may have something to do with the country's rather peculiar elongated pear shape, or it may even reflect the weakness of northern Austrians' regional pride. However, it is most likely related to the fact that Austria has no geopolitical center. The Alps and the Danube Valley divide the country into two unequal and distinct parts, and the federal capital of Vienna is far off-center in the East. For the residents of Vorarlberg, Vienna and Paris are practically equidistant.

The Alps and the Danube are not just Austria's two most prominent geographical features. They represent different historical traditions, socio-economic structures, and, in the final analysis, states of mind. They have contributed to the development of the different regional identities and personality types. A quick look at any topographical map of Austria shows how the western and southern provinces are separated from each other by various ranges and ridges within the Alps. Nature has given each province the aura of God-given inviolability. Whenever a tunnel is completed in western Austria, people on each end make the same tongue-in-cheek remark: "Man should not join what God has separated."

Trachten from the Salzkammergut region around 1820...

In this respect, Austria's Alpine provinces are part of a divine order, and they are filled with, if not devout, at least God-fearing inhabitants. A cursory glance at any Austrian census report reveals that the percentage of Austrians who declare religious affiliation, predominantly Roman Catholicism, is higher in small communities than in larger urban centers and drops from West to East. Therefore, there is evidently a relationship between the height of the mountains and the amount of religious conviction in Austria.

Alpine religiosity is undoubtedly part of these provinces' strong rural and agricultural traditions. Farmers everywhere have always relied on their own hands and the grace of God to make a living, and due to the far from bountiful conditions in the Alps, farmers there always have been a particularly hard-working, God-fearing, and independent-minded breed.

The strength and diversity of Alpine traditions have been reinforced by the mountains themselves which have provided natural

. . . and Trachten as they are worn today.

barriers to innovation. In the olden days, Alpine horizons were not broad like the panoramic view from a mountain top but tended to be as narrow and sheltered as the valleys that housed their residents. The mountains clearly defined a multitude of little worlds and ways of life. The only thing that changed fast in the Alps was the weather. Everything else had to literally and figuratively work its way uphill.

There are any number of examples for the variety of Alpine traditions. Each region, and in some cases each valley, has its own distinctive form of native dress called *Trachten,* and a trained eye can identify the home of a traditionally dressed Austrian by the color, material, pattern, and design of what he or she wears. The farmhouses in each province also have their own peculiar design and architectural features, and the Alpine sense of tradition, the way things have always been and therefore should be done, extends down to little things like how hay is dried. Here it is piled on a pole, there on a tripod, elsewhere on a rack.

However, many earthbound Alpine traditions have deteriorated to a great extent. This trend is not just an inevitable side-effect of modernization, mass communication, or "progress." Tourism has commercialized the splendid isolation of the Alps and completely changed the Alpine way of life. Internationally renowned ski centers like Lech, Kitzbühel, or Sankt Anton once were remote Alpine villages. Now they are the places to see and be seen in winter, filled with celebrities of all sorts ranging from European nobility to politicians, sports stars, millionaires, and social climbers. Where one skis in Austria is an implicit sign of having or wanting a certain amount of social prestige.

Many regions in the Alps practically live from tourism and now have all the sophisticated accoutrements of the modern leisure industry. *Trachten* nowadays not only refers to native dress but also is a branch of the clothing industry marketing the *"Trachten*-Look;" the village *Gasthaus* or inn may have a disco downstairs; renting a few rooms to tourists has become an indispensable source of income for many farmers; and the hay baler has made drying hay on a pole somewhat of an anachronism.

In spite of these innovations, the geography of Austria still divides *homo austriacus* into two generic groups: *homo alpinus,* the western and southern mountain people, and *homo danubius,* the valley people along the Danube. Alpine Austrians can be subdivided into species which correspond roughly to each mountain province, and within each province there is a complicated system of subspecies which makes it possible to distinguish the inhabitants of one valley from the next. Consequently there is a certain innate rivalry among the provinces as well as within them. However, within a given province, any natural antipathy between different regions or even rural and urban dwellers immediately disappears if that province is compared to another. Each province has its own sense of heritage, a provincial form of patriotism which can reach the point of being a tribal sensibility.

Unlike the Alps, which have always separated provinces and defined regions within them, the Danube River has joined and dominated its provinces. The variety of Danubian Austrians is less extensive than in the Alps partially because the landscape of the Danube Valley has provided fewer geographical niches and therefore never promoted such a high degree of differentiation. Certainly the inhabitants of the Alps in the provinces of Upper and Lower Austria have

An old photograph of Austrian "Bergbauern" (mountain-farmers) at work on marginally productive soil in the Alps; an endagered subspecies of homo alpinus.

some similarities with *homo alpinus,* but they lack the geocentric attitude that is one of the characteristic traits of the Alpine Austrian. There is a simple physical explanation for this. Most of the valleys on the northern slopes of the Alps in Upper and Lower Austria empty into the Danube Valley which is a non-Alpine point of orientation and always has drawn Upper and Lower Austrian mountain people into a broader stream of events.

With the sole exception of the Roman *Limes*, the Danube never has served as a natural frontier in Austria. It always has been Europe's most important thoroughfare to and from the Balkan and the Orient. Because eastern Austrians have inhabited a basically open landscape, they have been exposed to all the benefits and dangers that accompany the absence of natural barriers, and they do not seem to have the same sense of self-sufficiency or security which characterizes *homo alpinus*. God gave western Austrians the mountains to protect them. The wide open spaces of Lower Austria, Burgenland, or southern Styria may also have been part of a divine plan – to test the faith of their inhabitants with scourges like the Turks.

The sense of provincial tradition and self-esteem in eastern Austria also do not appear to be as strong or as passionate as in the West or the South. One explanation for this has to do with the political evolution of different agricultural traditions. The farmers in the West, for example, were freed from medieval practices like serfdom centuries before their counterparts in the East. They consequently developed a feeling of self-esteem and pride as "free farmers" which distinguished them from the farmers in the East, who were still caught in the bonds of subservience. The sheer size and different structure of the cities in the Danube Valley, Linz and Vienna in particular, also played a certain role in how people in the rural areas perceived themselves.

The concentration of business, trade, and industry in Linz and Vienna made the contours of the urban-rural contrast much sharper than in the Alps (with the noteable exception of the heavily industrialized areas in the Mürz and Mur Valleys in Upper Styria). Austria's provincial capitals outside of the East — Bregenz, Innsbruck, Salzburg, Klagenfurt, and even Graz — are urban without being metropolitan. They somehow allow the residents of their provincial hinterlands to feel comfortable when visiting, but the city folks in the Danube Valley always let farmers know that they considered them country bumpkins. This feeling of urban superiority was — and to a certain extent still is — particularly crass in Vienna because everyone who was not Viennese was seen as a country bumpkin. The relationship of Vienna to the provinces of its Danubian hinterland in the East as well as the Austrian provinces in general always has been rather strained. One of the few common denominators of Austria's diverse provincial traditions is a long-standing aversion for Vienna.

Vienna and the Provinces

There are two common fallacies about Austria. One is that Vienna represents the quintessence of Austria, and the other is that the provinces do. There are arguments in favor of both, but this kind of debate is similar to trying to ascertain which part of an egg is more important, the white or the yolk. Understanding Austria involves thinking in terms of Vienna *and* the provinces instead of Vienna *or* the provinces, even though the latter formulation perhaps more accurately captures the attitudes prevailing in Austria after World War I — some of which are still evident today.

In our days of mass communication and rapid transportation, it is difficult to imagine what it once meant for a provincial Austrian to visit Vienna, a city of some two million that was the political, bureaucratic, and economic hub of an empire of over fifty million. A journey to the imperial capital and residence frequently had all the characteristics of a once-in-a-lifetime pilgrimage reserved for a chosen few. Vienna was an imperial Mecca for the average man.

The city not only impressed provincial visitors with its sheer size or the architectural beauty of its monuments, ranging from St. Stephen's Cathedral and the imperial residence of the *Hofburg* to the series of monumental buildings along the *Ringstrasse*, the magnificent boulevard that encircles the inner city. The ethnic and cultural diversity of Vienna, a Central European melting pot which had attracted people from all nations and walks of life from throughout the empire, inevitably struck the provincial visitor, and this exoticism was not merely a matter of optical impressions.

There are, for example, great differences not only among Austria's various provincial dialects but also between them and the Viennese dialect. Viennese dialect is peppered with foreign expressions which have a variety of different social and national origins. There are borrowings from French, the language of aristocracy and diplomacy, as well as Yiddish, the German-Hebrew hybrid spoken by Eastern European Jews. *Vis-à-vis*, the French prepositional phrase meaning "across from," is just as common in Vienna as the German *gegenüber*, and *Zores*, the Yiddish expression for worries or troubles, is frequently used. The Turkish sieges also left a few linguistic marks on the city. *Schabraken*, a Viennese expression for an ugly old woman, comes from the Turkish *csparak*: saddle-blanket. A multitude of other examples can be cited from the other languages of the multinational empire such as Italian, Czech, or Hungarian or traced back to medieval German or Latin roots. Viennese dialect reflects the city's position between the Occident and the Orient and embodies its tradition of multinational assimilation.

In spite of the cultural diversity of Austria's provinces, ethnically they were extremely homogeneous in comparison to Vienna. In 1890, 65% of the residents of Vienna were not Viennese-born, the largest group being lower-class immigrants of Czech origin. The Slavic touch which resulted from this influx may be one of the explanations for the melancholy of the eastern Austrian in general, and the Viennese in particular, a trait diametrically opposed to Alpine assertiveness. The Viennese and the *homo alpinus* respond differently to the same situations. If a problem arises, the former tends to resign by saying: *Da kann ma nix machen.* ("There is nothing we can do.") The latter tends to criticize or assume responsibility: *Es ist höchste Zeit...* ("It is high time...")

The social structure of Vienna also was radically different from that of provincial cities. The six-hundred year presence of the Habsburg court had made Vienna an imperial center of political and economic power with a highly differentiated social hierarchy. Vienna attracted the aristocracy of blood and, in the course of the 19th century, the grand bourgeois aristocracy of wealth. It had a huge number of bureaucrats and servants, a small middle class, and a growing populace of proletarians who lived and worked under squalid conditions. The city's Jewish population was also large. In 1910, 8.6% of the Viennese, 170,000 residents, were Jews, and Vienna was second only to Warsaw in Europe in terms of the size of its Jewish community. (After 1918, Austria's Jews resided almost exclusively in Vienna.)

All of these features provided strong contrasts to the simpler and more straightforward provincial forms of society. Certainly there were rigid social hierarchies in the provinces, too, but they were less complicated. Rural and middle-class values tended to predominate in the provinces where there was a stronger sense of egalitarianism based on the idea of equality among peers. This attitude had little to do with the principles of democracy, but in the country people who considered themselves equals dealt with one another with a certain ease. Even today, provincial visitors in Vienna feel uncomfortable with the complexity of manners and customs there, and some of them find the famous charm of the Viennese contrived, insincere, or even servile.

Looking over the roof-tops of Vienna towards St. Stephen's Cathedral.

The provincial image of Vienna consisted of an ambivalent set of impressions which one young man from Upper Austria characterized in the following manner: "Dazzling riches and loathsome poverty alternated sharply... The court with its glamour... prostitution... liberal attitudes... Social Democrats... I was repelled by the conglomeration of races which the capital showed me, repelled by this whole mixture of Czechs, Poles, Hungarians, Ruthenians, Serbs, and Croats, and everywhere... Jews and more Jews. To me the giant city seemed the embodiment of racial desecration." These were some of the things which struck the eighteen-year-old Adolf Hitler when he came to Vienna in 1907. In *Mein Kampf,* Hitler's autobiographical outline of Nazi ideology, he looked back and called Vienna "the hardest, though most thorough, school of my life," a school that was essential in forming his world-view.

The Viennese, of course, viewed themselves differently. They were products of national interbreeding and cultural exchange on all levels, and heterogeneity was part and parcel of their heritage and way of life. They also enjoyed the centuries-old predominance of their city and had a tendency to bask in the limelight of imperial glory. Even today, some Viennese still refer to people from the provinces as G'scherte, a condescending reference that goes back centuries to when farmers had shorn (geschert) heads and could be easily identified as country bumpkins.

The collapse of the empire affected Vienna immediately and more drastically than it did the provinces, which at least had a certain degree of economic self-sufficiency and a sense of tradition they could fall back on. Vienna was an imperial-sized capital which lost its empire practically overnight. Geographically stranded on the easternmost tip of the Alpine foothills, it was much too large for the small state it was to rule. The provinces had traditionally not supplied Vienna, where almost one-third of Austria's population lived. The sheer structural incompatibility of Austria's over-sized capital with its underdeveloped provinces and the dire immediate post-war situation brought a number of traditional Viennese-provincial conflicts to a head.

The provinces hesitated to deliver anything to Vienna because they had their own problems, and Vienna had nothing to offer them in return, with the exception of a hopelessly inflated and worthless currency. By 1922, the Austrian crown had 1/15,000th of its pre-war value. Due to drastic shortages of coal and food, many Viennese reverted to foraging, scavenging, and barter as a means of survival. The Vienna Woods became a source of heating material, and the farmers of Lower Austria did a booming business on the black market trading food for silverware, furs, rugs, or anything else of value the city slickers had to offer, a practice which reversed traditional feelings of superiority. It was the farmers' turn to treat the Viennese with scorn.

The attitude of the provinces to Vienna was symptomatic of the lack of unity which prevailed in Austria right after the war. One explanation for the absence of national cohesiveness at that time was that the provinces (with the exception of Burgenland) pre-dated the foundation of the republic by centuries. Therefore, they initially did not accept the unity of Austria as a matter of fact. The Habsburgs not only had held the various nations of the empire together, but also, to a great extent, the German-speaking provinces which became Austria. Once the emperor disappeared, the provinces thought in provincial instead of national terms.

Vorarlberg, for example, drafted a provincial constitution which asserted its independence and sovereignty. Austria's westernmost province viewed its relationship to the federal republic as provisional, and it entered into negotiations with Switzerland about becoming a Swiss canton after 80% of the populace had mandated the government to do so in a plebiscite in 1919.

Tyrol also regarded its relationship to the republic as tentative and entertained the idea of founding a free, independent, and neutral state of Tyrol as a means of preventing the impending division of Tyrol at the Paris Peace Conference in 1919. After the Treaty of Saint-Germain made the loss of South Tyrol a matter of fact, there was a broad popular movement in Tyrol for a provincial Anschluss with Germany. This aspiration culminated in a plebiscite in 1921 in which over 90% of the populace voted for abandoning Austria. (The whole idea was futile because the victorious powers never would have allowed it.) Similar, if less pronounced, tendencies existed in the other Alpine provinces as well, and divergent provincial attitudes were merely reinforced by ideological differences throughout the country.

Red, Black, and Blue Politics

Austrians can define various periods of their history in terms of color combinations. The Babenbergs' dynastic colors were red-white-red, and the Habsburgs' imperial ones were black and yellow. In 1918, the Republic of Austria adopted red-white-red as its national colors because they were historically Austrian but without imperial associations.

Austria's political spectrum also has a tradition of color coordination. Red obviously belongs to the Austrian left with its strong socialist and weak communist traditions. Opponents of the conservatives identified them with black, the color of priests' robes which stood for clericalism and Roman Catholicism. German nationalists associated themselves with a light cornflower blue. However, the three political catchwords of the First Republic were red, black, and national, the latter being responsible for preventing a historically consistent political color scheme. Before 1918, the German nationalists in Austria embraced the black-red-gold of the Second German Reich, and during the interwar period many of them drifted from their own light blue to the brown associated with the Nazis' Third Reich.

When discussing Austria's political traditions, historians and political scientists seldom limit themselves to the topic of political parties. They use a much broader term which reflects the militant atmosphere and attitudes which prevailed in interwar Austria, "camps" (Lager). The three political camps divided Austria's political spectrum into distinct parts, and each camp had its own well-defined geographical and social bases of support.

Like the provinces, Austria's political parties and movements predated the foundation of the republic. They were part of Austria's imperial heritage. They also had a common ancestor to a certain extent, Austrian liberalism around 1870 — 1880, because the three personalities, who could be called the organizational "founding fathers" of the camps, all began their political carriers as liberals: the Social Democrat, Victor Adler (1852 — 1918), a physician from a wealthy Jewish family who embraced the cause of the masses; Karl Lueger (1844 — 1910), a lawyer of lower-class origins and advocate of the "little man," who was mayor of Vienna from 1896 to 1910 and a leading figure in the Christian Social movement; and Georg von Schönerer (1842 — 1921), a German-National and self-proclaimed "Teutonic knight" who fought for the cultural and racial purity of German-ness in the multinational empire. (It is important to distinguish between the term German-National, which refers to a camp on the right wing of the Austrian political spectrum, and the much broader concept of German nationalism.)

When the second half of the 19th century began, the liberals were the Habsburgs' main political opponents. Predominantly representatives of Austria's small and well educated upper-middle and upper classes, they fought against aristocratic privilege, political neo-absolutism, and clerical tutelage and promoted the democratic causes of individual freedom and rights as well as representative democracy. One of their greatest political achievements, the Constitution of 1867, paved the way for the laissez faire blossom of economic liberalism, which changed the face of the empire and created the social basis for the mass political movements in Austria. The achievements of free enterprise, big business, banking, and industry helped create the large urban working class from which the Social Democratic Party was to emerge, and they jeopardized the values and existence of the urban petty bourgeois and small rural farmers who were the backbone of the Christian Social movement. As a political doctrine which basically served the economic interests of the upper classes, Austrian liberalism failed to deal effectively with the social and structural problems it had created and hence increasingly forfeited credibility. With each extension of the right to vote — universal male suffrage was not introduced in the Austrian half of the monarchy until 1907 — the liberals lost influence.

As a set of enlightened, tolerant, and urbane attitudes, liberalism survived the political demise of the liberal movement to a certain extent, and a liberal spirit prevailed in places like the university, upper echelons of the imperial bureaucracy, and among artists, writers, and the well educated. Certain aspects of liberalism's political heritage were present in each of the political camps. Secular anticlericalism served as common denominator for the Social Democrats and the German-Nationals, and the Christian Socials and the German-Nationals both fundamentally accepted the idea of a liberal economic order. The German-Nationals also viewed themselves as heirs to the liberal tradition, insofar as the designations liberal-national, or national-liberal were used, but the spirit of German nationalism overshadowed the liberalism in the German-National camp. In any case, the ideological differences among the camps were much greater than any existing liberal affinities.

Adler, who unified the Austrian working class movement under the auspices of the Social Democratic Workers Party in 1888—1889, drew his theoretical inspiration from Marx and Engels, and "Austro-Marxists" rejected the principles of capitalism altogether which threatened the very foundations of the Christian Socials' and German-Nationals' world-views.

Lueger joined the Christian Social movement in the early 1880's, and rapidly became one of its leading spokesmen. He was inspired by the political program of Catholic social reform which presented itself an an alternative to the "extremes" of atheistic socialism and unfettered liberal capitalism. Particularly attractive to Roman Catholics and the "little man," the Christian Social movement appealed to its followers' religious convictions and economic interests.

Georg von Schönerer completely abandoned the liberal principles of tolerance and equality, absolutely rejected Roman Catholicism along with the catholicity of the Old-Austrian idea, and propagated a racial theory of German nationalism which was virulently anti-Slavic and anti-semitic.

One of the peculiarities of the Austrian political spectrum was that there was practically no area of transition between the socialists on the left and the Christian Social movement right of center, which basically allied itself with the German-Nationals on the right against the socialists. As a secular and anti-clerical, but capitalistic doctrine, Austrian liberalism could have filled the gap between the secular and anti-clerical, but anti-capitalistic, Social Democrats on the left and the capitalistic but religiously motivated Christian Social movement right of center. However, by 1918 the Social Democrats and Christian Socials had the masses in their wakes, and the German-Nationals, a loose confederation of different groups approximately half of the size of either of the mass parties, also had a firm following. This constellation created a slight but critical imbalance between the left and the right, and the absence of a center party that could mediate between the extremes made Austria a "land without a middle."

The political tri-polarity of red, black, and German-National Austrians juxtaposed onto the other structural, regional, and social polarities of Austria is one of the keys to understanding the country's political culture. Up until 1918, the conflicts among the three political camps were muted to a certain extent by the emperor and the imperial order which served as containing forces and common obstacles, but when the emperor and the empire disappeared, an unprecedentedly open, democratic forum of political conflict emerged, the First Republic.

Germans and Jews

The collapse of the Habsburg Empire definitely affected the status of Jews in Austria. Before 1918, they were one of the multinational empire's many minorities, but after 1918 they assumed the status of the most prominent minority in a state which considered itself "German." However, very few Jews in Austria felt anti-semitism was an existential threat before or after 1918, an assumption which proved to be a fatal misconception after the Nazi occupation of Austria in 1938.

Austrian anti-semitism is frequently viewed in a different light than anti-semitism elsewhere. Even though Hitler considered himself a German and despised the idea of Austria, he was Austrian born and raised. He spent the formative years of his youth, 1907–1913, in Vienna and favorably mentioned politicians like Karl Lueger and Georg von Schönerer in *Mein Kampf*. Nevertheless, its is important to distinguish among at least three different anti-semitic traditions, which influenced Hitler, and his genocidal scheme of the "final solution." Equating the former with the latter is just as problematic as gross generalizations about Austrian anti-semitism.

Up until the second half of the 19th century, the German-speaking parts of the Austrian empire had relatively small Jewish populations which were mainly concentrated in the urban centers of contemporary eastern Austria. As a fundamentally Roman Catholic country, Austria had a long anti-semitic tradition which reached back to the Middle Ages. This form of religiously motivated anti-semitism was particularly strong in areas where the population was traditionally devout, but Jews had rarely lived, like the Alps.

The development of a second, so-called economic form of anti-semitism began after 1867 when liberal constitutional reforms granted equality to all citizens. The acquisition of a basic right, the freedom of movement, allowed Jews to emigrate from the ghettos of the eastern part of the empire to urban centers in the west like Vienna, Prague, or Budapest. In Vienna, for example, the Jewish population rose from 6,200 (2.2%) to 175,000 (8.6%) between 1860 and 1910. Mostly newcomers from the East, Vienna's Jews were spread across the social spectrum, from businessmen and bankers to panhandlers and paupers, and they were perceived as a two-fold economic threat. On the one hand, the lower-class Jewish immigrants provided a new and unwanted source of competition for the indigenous small businessmen. On the other hand, there was a well educated, predominantly liberal, and influential group of assimilated Jews in Vienna, and, in terms of their relative percentage of the total population, they were overrepresented in professional fields like law, medicine, and academics, as well as in journalism, merchandising, and finance.

Demagogic politicians took these Jews and made them exclusively responsible for certain ideological and economic interests. Coining phrases like "the Jewish-liberal press" and "Jewish capital," they identified "the Jew" as the enemy of every hard-working and God-fearing "little man." For representatives of this petty bourgeois form

85

Orthodox Eastern European Jews from Galicia in Vienna around the turn of the century.

of anti-semitism, "Jew" was synonymous with promiscuous liberalism and unfettered capitalism, phenomena which threatened the values and interests of the average middle-class citizen.

Karl Lueger recognized the political potential of anti-semitism and ruthlessly exploited it. There are a number of circumstances, however, which seem to indicate that Lueger principally viewed anti-semitism as an effective, pragmatic means of attracting and organizing a following, rather than as a political end in itself. On this basis, some historians argue that Lueger was not a representative of racial anti-semitism, which does not absolve him of the responsibility for helping create an atmosphere in which racial anti-semitism flourished. However, it is an attempt to break an ideological nexus which is sometimes established between the Christian Social tradition and

National Socialism. There is no getting around the fact that Lueger demagogically used anti-semitism, especially early in his political career, but a blanket condemnation of the Christian Social movement as proto-Nazi is historically untenable. Lueger's anti-semitism also frequently overshadows his achievements as a communal politician who was responsible for a series of social projects and programs which undoubtedly benefited all Viennese.

The last phase in the development of Austrian anti-semitism began towards the end of the 19th century. At that time in Europe, there was an abundance of scientifically unfounded but popularly digestible theories about physiognomical, psychological, and cultural types which were based on the concept of race. These theories attributed the success of a particular race or nation to its "natural" traits and its ability to maintain its purity by not interbreeding with inferior races possessing less innate intelligence, character, strength, beauty, etc. Among German-Nationals in Austria, this kind of racial theory was popularly accepted because Austrian multinationality was seen by them as a prime example of degeneration. German nationalistic theories of racial types were obsessed with the concept of the purity of the German *Volk*, and they borrowed prejudices from the religious and economic traditions of anti-semitism to make "the Jew" the epitome of degeneration and evil.

The degree of anti-semitism in Austria increased from left to right on the political spectrum. Although lowest among Social Democrats, whose party elite included a great number of intellectuals with Jewish backgrounds, there were nevertheless some members of the working class who adopted the demagogic identification of the capitalist with the Jew. Some members of the Christian Social and German-National camps added a new anti-semitic element to their anti-Marxism by equating "the Jew" with "the Marxist." After all, Marx as well as many leading figures throughout the European left had Jewish heritages: Victor Adler, the founding father of the Social Democratic Party, and Otto Bauer, the party's chairman and leading theoretician in the First Republic, were good local examples. This new twist of argument made "the Jew" a perfect all-purpose enemy and scapegoat simultaneously responsible for the Marxian-socialist and the liberal-capitalist versions of godless materialism, an interpretation which some clerics all too readily propagated. There were, however, Christian Socials who had great reservations about this kind of primitive stereotyping. The intensity and frequency of racial anti-semitism was without a doubt greatest among the German-Nationals on the right.

After 1938, the Nazis drove out or destroyed Austria's Jewish population almost completely. In spite of the fact that Austria's Jewish population is very small today — about 9,000 — a phenomenon called "anti-semitism without Jews" can be observed. Since very few Austrians acknowledge being anti-semitic, this situation has been circumscribed as "anti-semitism without anti-semites," that is, anti-semites in the public and political sense of the term. Contemporary anti-semitism is much more discrete and elusive than its historical predecessors, but Austria still has a reputation for being a traditionally anti-semitic country. This type of accusation is a bit oversimplified.

There are fundamentally two different ways of viewing anti-semitism in Austria. Observers adopting a historical perspective positively stress that the amount of anti-semitism in Austria has dropped enormously since the interwar period or World War II; however, critics are quick to point out that there still is much too much anti-semitism in Austria. Social scientists estimate that anywhere between 7 and 10% of the populace can be considered hard-core anti-semites, but it is important to make a few distinctions here.

Anti-semitic attitudes are more prevalent among older generations than younger ones, an indication that anti-semites are literally dying out in Austria, or that their attitudes are not being adopted by their offspring to a great extent. There is also a correlation between educational levels or professional groups and anti-semitic attitudes, which are less pronounced among the better educated or white-collar employees than they are among the less educated, farmers and the self-employed. Last of all, there are regional differences in the amount of anti-semitism in Austria which reflect traditional political preferences as well as geography. Anti-semitic attitudes increase from left to right on the political spectrum and from East to West in Austria. Lowest in the large urban centers in the Danube Valley like Vienna and Linz or among socialists, anti-semitic sentiments tend to increase in the South and the West as the communities get smaller, the mountains get higher, or as the conservative and German-national political traditions get stronger. For example, an Alpine farmer with a low level of education is less predisposed to change his attitudes, regardless of what they are, than a better educated or more liberal thinking urban dweller.

It would be unfair to categorize Austria's *homo alpinus* as an anti-semite — Vorarlberg's low incidence of anti-semitism, for example, is an exception to the Alpine rule — but there is a relationship between the strength of traditional attitudes in Austria and the frequency of anti-semitism. Austrians' responses to being confronted with their country's anti-semitism may range from embarrassment or self-criticism to defensive aggressiveness. Apologists attempt to trivialize anti-semitism just as some critics are prone to exaggerate it, but in any event it is a tradition upon which time and education slowly and fortunately are taking their toll.

5. The First Republic:
The State No One Wanted

Austria's First Republic has been called "the state no one wanted." Austrian and foreign politicians had severe doubts about the viability of Austria, but even more severe were the doubts Austrians had about each other. One of the prominent characteristics of the political life of the First Republic was the "camp mentality," an ideologically motivated us-versus-them attitude which spread suspicion instead of trust and undermined the preparedness for the day-to-day give-and-take which is so necessary in the democratic process. Conflict among the camps was not limited to the traditional arenas of politics: from 1918 to 1938, the victims of politically related violence in Austria totaled over 800 dead and 2,000 injured.

Austrians' political preferences and conflicts mirrored the country's existing geographical and social distinctions, and the history of the First Republic was in many respects an ideologically colored struggle between *homo alpinus* and *homo danubius* or the "black provinces" and "Red Vienna." The Christian Socials' strengths were in the mountains of the West and the South, whereas the Social Democrats' support was in the valleys of the East along the Danube and in Upper Styria. The Christian Socials drew their support from rural areas and from the urban lower-middle-class on up, whereas the Social Democrats had an almost exclusively urban working-class following. As practicing Catholics, the Christian Socials believed in traditional values and the established social order, whereas the predominantly irreligious Social Democrats embraced the idea of revolutionary change. Each of the major parties had highly organized followings which strongly identified themselves with their respective ideologies. (In spite of the various changes in Austria's social structure, some regional shifts in power, and a tempering of ideologies since World War II, the domestic East-West political alignment of Austria has remained fundamentally the same to date.)

There was, however, some competition between the Christian

Socials and the German-Nationals. Sprinkled throughout the country, the German-Nationals were especially well represented in the Carinthian and Styrian borderlands—in some respects a belated consequence of the border conflicts with the Yugoslavs — or they recruited followers from well-educated and prosperous liberal circles that traditionally had been inclined to German nationalism. Nonetheless, the common denominator of anti-Marxism drew the Christian Socials and German-Nationals into an uneasy alliance against the left.

The Two-and-a-Half Party System

In spite of the conflicts among the camps, the first few years of the First Republic were marked by the sheer necessity of political cooperation. Making a virtue of necessity, the parties realized they had to get the republic on its feet and shared the task of governing Austria together in a coalition from 1918 to 1920. In February 1919, elections were held for the so-called "Constitutional National Assembly," a representative body or "constitutional congress" responsible for shaping the state. None of the parties achieved an absolute majority of seats, which were distributed in the following manner: seventy-two Social Democrats, sixty-nine Christian Socials, twenty-six German-Nationals, and one Communist. (The Communist Party of Austria was founded on November 12, 1918, the same day the Republic of Austria was proclaimed.)

These results reflect in many respects Austrians' electoral behavior to the present day. Although their relative strengths have varied, the two major parties have always accumulated at least 80% of the votes; the working classes have remained loyal to the socialist movement, which has made the communists a negligible factor in domestic politics; and, excluding an absolute majority or cooperation between the two major parties, the smaller third camp has been in a position to determine which major party comes to power. In terms of the sizes of the parties and their relationships to each other, Austria's First Republic was effectively a two-and-one-half party system. Neither of the major parties achieved an absolute majority in the interwar period, and from 1920 onward, the Christian Socials relied on coalitions with a variety of smaller parties on the right to stay in pow-

A caricature by Ironimus portraying the constituencies and relative sizes of Austria's three political camps (l. to r.): a socialist blue-collar worker, a conservative dressed in an Alpine "Trachten," and a proportionately smaller representative of the liberal-national camp.

er. This constellation made the smallest representative group disproportionately important.

The drafting of the Austrian constitution, which was ratified in October 1920, reflected the parties' different interests and regional strengths. The parties reached a general consensus rather quickly to avoid two extremes: a strong presidential office, on the one hand, and an all-too-loose confederation of basically autonomous provinces, on the other. However, one of the central points of contention among the parties was the division of competences and rights between the federal government and the provinces; that is, how centralized or decentralized political power was to be.

The Social Democrats favored a high degree of centralization, which reflected their interest in a federal government that would be able to dictate progressive legislation over the heads of the conservative provinces. They also advocated a unicameral legislature based on proportional representation, a democratic principle which reflected their strength in the larger urban population centers.

The Christian Socials, on the other hand, were interested in maintaining as many rights and as much autonomy for those areas in which they were strongest but the population was thinnest, the provinces. They proposed a bicameral parliament in which the provinces would be equally represented in a second chamber, regardless of the size of their populations. With this proposal, the Christian Socials hoped to offset the strength of the Social Democrats in the large population centers similar to the manner in which the US Senate offsets the House of Representatives.

The constitution that was drafted had all the characteristics of a compromise. It provided for a weak president with representative functions and a bicameral parliament consisting of a strong national chamber, the *Nationalrat*, and a weaker provincial chamber, the *Bundesrat*, which was only equipped with a suspensive veto enabling it to send legislation back to the *Nationalrat*. This solution may appear to be a bicameral answer to the Social Democrats' demands for a strong federal legislature and the conservatives' desire to control the same, but due to the stability and rigidity of the political alignment throughout the country, it was effectively unicameral in practice. The division of seats in the provincial legislatures *(Landtage)* and both chambers of the federal parliament were practically identical because the camp mentality hardly allowed for distinctions between provincial and national politics.

The adoption of the system of proportional representation for the *Nationalrat* and the provincial legislatures also had the unintended and unfortunate consequence of reinforcing the camp mentality within the electoral process itself. The system of proportional representation is based on assigning seats according to the percentage of votes each party receives. For example, if there are ten seats in an electoral district, each party submits a list of ten candidates, and citizens vote for one of the party lists. After the ballots are tallied, the seats are distributed among the parties according to the percentage of votes each list received. For example, 50 % of the votes for one list means that the first five candidates of that list receive seats; 30 % for the next list, three seats, etc.

This simple example by no means takes into account all of the complexities of electoral mathematics, but it does show to what extent proportional representation encourages citizens to vote for a party, an ideology, or a world-view instead of an individual candidate or personality, as is the case in a head-to-head, winner-take-all electoral system. Given the high degree of party organization and peoples' strong sense of ideological commitment in the First Republic, there were very few "independents" who changed their political preferences from one election to the next, a phenomenon which can be observed in Austria today along with the fact that Austrians still tend to vote for parties instead of personalities.

Red Vienna and the Black Provinces

Very few tourists go out of their way to visit the monuments of "Red Vienna" (Rotes Wien): gigantic interwar communal housing projects which are well off the beaten path of obligatory imperial attractions. Vienna was the first major city in the world to be managed by a socialist municipal administration, and ever since 1919 each of its freely elected mayors as well as the majority of its city councils have been socialist. Historically the capital of Lower Austria, the drafting of the constitution made the city a province in its own right, and Vienna was the only province in the First Republic where the Social Democrats had a majority. This exception merely added a new ideological dimension to the traditional antipathies between Vienna and the provinces.

The Social Democrats withdrew from the coalition with the conservative parties in 1920 for ideological and tactical reasons. On the one hand, the Social Democrats' cooperation with the "representatives of capitalism" had been an uneasy marriage, and on the other, they thought letting the conservative coalition rule alone would increase their chances for winning an absolute majority in the near future, a goal which turned out to be illusory. In spite of the austerity measures of the conservatives in the twenties and the widespread economic hardships of the thirties, the Social Democrats remained isolated in Parliament as a large and vocal, but basically impotent party in the opposition. Excluded from the responsibility of decision-making on the national stage of politics, the Social Democrats took ample advantage of their supremacy in Vienna by introducing sweeping reforms.

During the interwar period, Red Vienna became an internationally recognized model of municipal management with a reputation for being a "Mecca of social welfare." One of the first problems the

"The Federal Capital of Vienna" by Ironimus. Austria from a distorted Viennese point of view: socialist Vienna (r.) and the conservative provinces (l.).

Social Democrats had to solve was finding a means of financing their ambitious programs. Hugo Breitner, a Social Democrat, former banker, assimilated Jew, and city councilman for finances, described his strategy for raising funds in a straightforward manner which also illustrates the tone of political discourse that prevailed in those days: "Not to be unnerved by all of the wailing and moaning of the tax-shy propertied class, we are going to get the money necessary for fulfilling the manifold tasks of the city where it really is to be found."

Before 1918, the city had generated most of its income through flat-rate indirect taxation on necessities like rent and food or municipally-owned utilities like water, gas, and electricity, which represented a disproportionately large burden for lower income groups. Breitner introduced the now commonplace, but then revolutionary practice of direct and progressive taxes, which affected the upper income groups in particular. For example, property, rents for larger "luxury" apartments, automobiles, horses, servants, entertainment, certain foods and drinks, were subject to new taxes. In other words, just about everything that was above and beyond the means of the average working-class family. These taxes naturally were unpopular with the conservatives who had to pay them, but they were an extremely effective means of raising direly needed income for the city.

Many of the city's social programs were directly or indirectly related to Vienna's housing problem. Before World War I, 73% of the Viennese lived in one or two room flats which had been hastily thrown up during the second half of the 19th century to accommodate the boom in the city's population. Often hopelessly overcrowded, these small and dingy quarters lacked the simplest conveniences. They were named after a common faucet in the hall, the *Bassena*, which was the only source of water for each floor.

The nourishment and living conditions of broad sections of the populace in Vienna were so miserable that tuberculosis was epidemic. Called the "Viennese illness" throughout Europe, tuberculosis was the cause of one out of seven "natural deaths" in Vienna before 1914, and one out of four during World War I. Given these circumstances, it is clear why two of the main thrusts of the municipal programs were health and housing.

From 1923 to 1933, over 350 apartment complexes, twenty-six of which were "superblocks" with over 800 units, were erected in the course of communal building projects *(Gemeindebauten)*, and 63,000 new apartments provided homes for almost a quarter of a million people. The apartments were small, but they were equipped with all the modern conveniences: gas, electricity, running water, and a toilet. (Showers were excluded because they could have been taxed as a luxury.) A combined result of financial and aesthetic considerations, the simple and sober apartment complexes were designed to provide their residents with as much fresh air and direct light as possible. The large courtyards, which resulted from this type of design, doubled as playgrounds and frequently housed municipal services like public baths, laundries, libraries, kindergartens, health clinics, or social workers' offices. Rents were low, the city assigned apartments according to social need, and the great majority of the needy were Social Democrats or politically so inclined. Red Vienna was particularly proud of its municipal apartment complexes, which were rhetorically stylized into being "palaces for the people"; the conservatives, however, tended to interpret them as symbols of collectivization and as fortresses for their enemies.

The Social Democrats introduced a tremendous number of other programs: school reforms, adult education programs, day-care and recreational facilities for children, health services, and the like. As examples of socialist values and organization, all of these innovations were buttressed by an all-encompassing idea of workers' or proletarian culture *(Arbeiterkultur)*.

The Social Democrats saw workers' culture as an alternative to the traditional, bourgeois, conservative capitalistic way of life and as a forerunner of the socialist society to come. This combination of political subculture and *avant-garde* attitudes led to a proliferation of party suborganizations that encompassed all stages and aspects of life. For example, the *Kinderfreunde* (Children's Friends) organized recreational activities for the young, and the *Roten Falken* (Red Falcons), complete with uniforms and an honor code, were an alternative to the "reactionary" Boy Scouts who were often housed in parish churches. The *Naturfreunde* (Friends of Nature) was a socialist outdoor and hiking club. There was a "red" automobile and cyclists' club, not to mention athletic clubs, orchestras, and choir groups. The Social Democrats founded the "Free Thinkers Union," an openly atheistic organization, and a special association with 100,000 members called "The Flame" promoted cremation as the progressive and socialist means of burial, a practice Catholics regarded as sacrilegious at that time.

Existing parallel to the established organizations of "conservative culture," but diametrically opposed to their values, Social Democratic suborganizations attempted to give the working class its own set of values and cultural identity. However, the idea of workers' culture had the negative side effect of transmitting the camp mentality from the arena of party politics into practically all realms of life.

Some of the above-mentioned organizations re-emerged in Austria after World War II without formal party affiliations, but with strong historical associations. Nowadays many Austrians have a tendency to think of organizations in terms of "red" and "black." Some conservatives use the terminology "independent" and "red" which is justified insofar as many of the organizations dominated by conservatives in the interwar period had no formal party affiliation. However, they overlook the fact that many of the former "red" organizations now are no longer party affiliated. Some socialists still use the old red-and-black terminology. These expressions are remnants of the interwar camp vocabulary and mentality.

"Clean up: Vote Social Democratic," a campaign poster from 1920 portraying the Austro-Marxists' perception of their political tasks. At the feet of the Social Democratic worker (l. to r.): a landowner, a banker, the Habsburgs' throne on top of a pile of war material, a priest, and an army officer.

The philosophy behind Red Vienna and workers' culture, Austro-Marxism, was a hybrid of Marxist theory and democratic principles which coupled the ideas of class struggle and revolutionary change with the conviction that the politically organized masses could radically transform the state and society without violence and bloodshed. Critics of Austro-Marxism from the left and the right found this combination implausible. Some conservatives, for example, abhored the Marxist revolutionary vocabulary of the Social Democrats, dismissed their democracy as a mere tactical ploy, and labeled their philosophy "Austro-Bolshevism." Real Bolshevists like Lenin, however, dismissed the Austro-Marxists as "petty bourgeois democrats" or even "accomplices" of the bourgeoisie in view of their commitment to democratic institutions and procedures. For the conservatives, the Social Democrats were revolutionary wolves in democratic sheep's clothing and for the communists democratic sheep in revolutionary wolf's clothing. The latter metaphor is perhaps a more accurate description of the paradox inherent in Austro-Marxism's coupling of revolutionary theory with democratic practice.

One of the fatal characteristics of political life in interwar Austria was that the conservatives took the Social Democrats' revolutionary rhetoric at face value. The Social Democrats, in turn, tended to view the coalition on the right as a monolithic, reactionary "bourgeois bloc." They hardly differentiated between the democratic and antidemocratic elements there, an attitude which only gradually became justified in the thirties as the anti-democratic forces gained the upper hand on the right.

One of the Social Democrats' interwar campaign slogans was: "From Red Vienna to Red Austria." Red Vienna represented everything the Social Democrats believed in and everything the conservatives feared. In this respect, the great experiment in socialist communal management merely contributed to the political polarization of the First Republic by showing the conservatives exactly what would happen in Austria if the Social Democrats ever were to achieve an absolute majority on a national level.

From Bad to Worse

One of the peculiarities of the First Republic was that Austria's army and police were not the only armed organizations in the country. Each of the political camps had paramilitary followings, private armies so to speak, which emerged from the chaos of 1918 as initially useful organizations but long outlived their utility to become permanent and fatal features of Austria's political landscape. After World War I, local *Heimwehr* (home defense) organizations sprang up throughout the country to compensate for the virtual collapse of the executive. They not only protected homes and property from marauding soldiers returning from the front, but also Austria itself in the borderlands of Carinthia, Styria, and Burgenland. In the cities, the Social Democrats organized armed workers and soldiers' councils responsible for maintaining public security. At that time, this task consisted of holding Austria's small but energetic Communist Party in check and defending democracy, which involved being prepared for the possibility of a restoration of the monarchy or a "counter-revolution" from the right. In the immediate postwar period, the state was too weak to disarm these groups, and the parties were too suspicious of each other to do it themselves.

Although some of the *Heimwehr* organizations had German nationalist inclinations, the majority of them were aligned with the Christian Social movement. In 1923, the Social Democrats formed their own paramilitary suborganization, the *Republikanische Schutzbund*, partially as a means of monopolizing the armed formations on the left and partially as a response to the threat they perceived in the *Heimwehr* on the right. Both the *Heimwehr* and the *Schutzbund* thought they were protecting the republic; the former from the possibility of a Bolshevik revolution in Austria and the latter from the prospect of a reactionary putsch that would destroy democracy.

Ideological hostility, political virility, and weekend exercises held by the paramilitary groups led regularly to bitter, but more or less harmless conflicts between these part-time "soldiers" that ended with "casualties" similar to those of barroom brawls. However, in January 1927 one of these altercations ended fatally. In the small village of Schattendorf in Burgenland, members of a local veterans' club fired into a group of *Schutzbund* members and supporters, killing a child and a war invalid, and wounding five others. Put on trial in Vienna for murder, the three accused pleaded self-defense and were acquitted on July 14, 1927 after a jury trial. Given the evidence — one of the victims had been shot in the back of the head — the acquittal was neither popular nor especially plausible.

The Social Democrats' response to this situation was ambivalent. On the one hand, the party leadership agreed that it would be unwise and undemocratic to protest the results of a jury trial, and they made the fatal mistake of avoiding a discussion of the entire affair with the enraged rank-and-file of the party. On the other hand, Frederick Austerlitz, the editor of the party's official newspaper, *Arbeiter-Zeitung*, wrote a flaming front page editorial that spoke of "workers' murderers," the absolute lack of justice for the proletariat in the "capitalistic order," and insinuated that the accused had been acquitted because they had killed workers. Actually intended to help the workers ventilate their anger, Austerlitz's rhetorical brilliance was taken at face value by many members of the rank-and-file who took things into their own hands the next day.

Thousands of indignant workers spontaneously marched on the inner city in a protest that was neither planned nor sanctioned by the Social Democratic Party and consequently lacked any semblance of organization or discipline. Each attempt of the police to break up the masses of protesters who milled around resulted in spiraling tempers and violence. Since the protesters really had no set goal, the Palace of Justice, next to the Parliament, arbitrarily became the victim of the workers' rage and was set on fire. Thousands of workers collected to watch the spectacular symbolic sacrifice which satisfied their need for revenge, and they initially refused to let the fire department through their ranks to squelch the flames.

The conservative government, convinced that the situation was completely out of control, decided that the only way to end this episode of mob rule was by force, and gave the police directives to use firearms to re-establish order. Just as the first fire engine made its way to the flaming building and the crowd began to disperse, police units appeared on the scene and repeatedly fired into the crowd of unarmed protesters. The day ended with 89 dead and 1,057 wounded. The great majority of casualties were workers. Only four of the fatalities were police.

The Schattendorf incident was a turning point from bad to worse in the history of the First Republic. The conduct of the protesting workers merely showed the conservatives what kind of violent potential slumbered in the Social Democratic "mob," and the measures of the conservative government and the police merely confirmed the Social Democrats' conviction that the bourgeois state was a reactionary instrument of capitalism for oppressing the proletariat. The parties lost confidence in each other's integrity and credibility, and their already scare willingness to cooperate evaporated.

After the Schattendorf incident, a number of ideological transformations began taking place in Austria. On the right wing of the

101

*"Rembember July 15,"
a joint Christian
Social-Heimwehr
campaign poster from
1930 reflecting their
perception of the
events on July 15,
1927: the burning
Palace of Justice over-
shadowed by a
wild-eyed, red arson
representing the
Social Democrats.*

Christian Social Party, the idea of replacing parliamentary democracy with a so-called "corporate" state under strong authoritarian
leadership became increasingly popular. Part of this idea was based
on doing away with political parties, a constant source of societal
conflict, and replacing them with an all-encompassing network of
organizations that would represent people not according to their
political convictions, but according to their occupational groups and
interests. Representatives from the chamber of agriculture, for
example, would advocate the farmers' interests; a union, the workers'; chambers of industry, trade, and commerce, each of those
branches, and so forth. The cooperative model of society was diametrically opposed to the Austro-Marxists' concept of class stuggle
just as the idea of an authoritarian corporate state contradicted the
Social Democrats' idea of democracy.

The Schattendorf incident also had the side effect of increasing the popularity of the *Heimwehr* movement throughout Austria, in rural areas in particular. Coming into its own as a political party, the *Heimwehr* movement swung out of the wake of the Christian Social Party and became a new factor on the right. The ideological and regional rivalries within the *Heimwehr* movement reflected its provincial origins and actually prevented it from formulating a coherent program or founding a strong central organization. Nevertheless, the *Heimwehr* was unified by its staunch anti-Marxism and open contempt for parliamentary democracy. They admired what Mussolini and fascism had done for Italy and wanted to do the same for Austria.

"Against Civil War – For Disarmament: Vote Social Democratic," the socialist portrayal of the same event: a working-class victim of the police actions, his mourning widow, and a terrified orphan.

Hitler's rise to power in Germany also directly affected Austria. More and more German-Nationals joined the ranks of Austria's Nazi Party, and after Hitler became chancellor of Germany in January 1933, he began pursuing an aggressively anti-Austrian course with the long term strategy of destroying Austrian independence with a Nazi Anschluss.

There was actually very little the Social Democrats could do about these developments on the right even though they emerged from the last free elections of the First Republic in 1930 with 41% of the votes as the largest party in Parliament. Still isolated in the opposition by a conservative coalition, they adopted a wait-and-see attitude. The economic hardships of the Great Depression—Austrian unemployment rose from 280,000 in 1929 to 600,000 in 1933—was bound to work to their advantage, and the crisis was seen as a sign of the impending collapse of capitalism that was to precede the establishment of socialism. Hitler's rise to power incidentally also influenced the Social Democrats' party program. Up until 1933, the Social Democrats had in many respects been the Anschluss party in Austria, but the transformation of Germany from a democracy into a Nazi regime made them drop this traditional goal.

The Politics of Fratricide

A turbulent session in Parliament on March 4, 1933 began a chain of events which led to the demise of democracy in Austria. All three of the Parliament's "presidents" — representatives from the parties responsible for presiding over the sessions — resigned which left Parliament with no one to call it to order or adjourn it, an unprecedented technical problem not covered by its rules of order. The conservative federal chancellor, Engelbert Dollfuss, took advantage of this situation by declaring that Parliament had "suspended itself" and used an outdated emergency powers act from 1917 as the pseudo-legal basis for ending parliamentary democracy in Austria. One of his first measures was to suspend the freedom of assembly, a move designed to keep the Social Democrats from marching in protest, and further curtailments of civil rights followed.

Within three months, Dollfuss banned the Communist Party, the Nazi Party, and the *Schutzbund*, which merely forced each of these organizations underground, and in September 1933 he founded an organization called the "Fatherland Front" which was intended to pool popular support for his authoritarian measures and draw the Austrian people together into one party.

Dollfuss also began to propagate a radically new Austrian ideology by rejuvenating aspects of the imperial Old-Austrian idea and reinterpreting them to apply to the small German state of Austria. Historically Austria had been a bulwark of Christian-German culture in Central Europe, and Dollfuss viewed Austria's political role in fundamentally the same terms. The contemporary threats were Bolshevism and Nazism.

As a Christian Social, Dollfuss had obvious reasons for rejecting Marxism. He based his critique of National Socialism on the historical unity of Christian and German culture and recognized that the Nazis had replaced the former with Teutonic paganism and perverted the latter with racism and terror. Using these criteria, Dollfuss viewed the Austrians as the better Germans, defenders of a thousand-year-old tradition, and he was actually the first prominent politician in interwar Austria to completely reject the Anschluss, promote an unprecedented version of Austrian patriotism, and affirm the idea of "Austrianness" (Österreichertum), a combination of tolerance and German culture: "Living with other nations for centuries has made the Austrian softer, more patient, and more understanding of foreign cultures, even though he has been and is conscious of maintaining the purity of his own culture and kind."

In dealing with his political opponents, Dollfuss hardly showed the Austrian tolerance he praised so lavishly. In one of his most famous programmatic speeches, held in September 1933, he stated his objectives: "We want a social, Christian, German state of Austria organized on a corporate basis with a strong authoritarian leadership." Having already banned the Nazi Party, the major obstacle blocking the realization of his political vision was the Social Democractic Party.

By February 1934, the relationship between the Dollfuss regime and the Social Democrats had reached a stand-off. Dollfuss had backed the Social Democrats into a corner, but he had not crossed the line they had drawn which would compel them to armed resistance. Ironically, the decision to fight was not made in Vienna by Dollfuss or the leadership of the Social Democrats. Austria's brief "civil war" was started by zealous subordinates from both camps in Linz.

Austrian authorities apprehending a member of the Social Democratic paramilitary organization, the "Schutzbund," in Linz on February 12, 1934.

On the morning of February 12, 1934, police broke down the doors of a Social Democratic workers' club in Linz to search it for weapons, and the local commander of the *Schutzbund* insubordinately acted against a directive from party headquarters in Vienna by giving orders to open fire. It was obvious that the Social Democrats had not planned a revolt, but after the first blood had been spilled on both sides, fighting spread like wildfire. For three days, members of the Social Democratic *Schutzbund* throughout Austria desperately fought not for a revolution but for the right of their party to exist, and they lost.

The heaviest fighting was concentrated in the industrial centers of the Mur and Mürz valleys in Upper Styria, the Danube Valley, and Vienna – socialists are not an Alpine but a valley phenomenon – but the *Schutzbund*, hopelessly outnumbered and underequipped in comparison to the combined forces of the Austrian army, the police, and the *Heimwehr*, really did not have a chance. In Vienna, the large communal building projects became what the conservatives always had suspected them of being, "fortresses," and the government used artillery on these *Schutzbund* positions to break resistance there in spite of the fact that they also housed women and children.

The official government statistics for the casualties from February 12 – 15 were 128 dead and 409 wounded for the executive and 137 dead and 399 wounded for the *Schutzbund*, whose casualities most likely were well over a thousand. Leading Social Democrats fled the country or were arrested, imprisoned, and in nine cases, executed. The victors banned the Social Democratic Party and all its suborganizations, and the socialists reorganized underground as the "Revolutionary Socialists." Austrian democracy ended with a political fratricide.

Comprehending contemporary Austrian politics at its best and its worst involves an adequate understanding of the attitudes and events which culminated in February 1934. Whenever Austria's conservatives and socialists have trouble resolving their differences today, the shadow of the First Republic suddenly looms up and admonishes them to cooperate. Nevertheless, when issues of principle or irreconcilable differences arise, traces of the old red-or-black camp mentality can poison the political atmosphere.

For example, in 1982 a socialist majority government refused to handle a conservative referendum that carried over 1.3 million signatures, a legitimate measure according to the rules of parliamentary democracy. As a result, some conservatives in Parliament questioned the socialist Federal Chancellor, Bruno Kreisky, about his "understanding of democracy." Losing his temper, Kreisky responded in the following manner: "Don't you doubt the understanding of democracy with a man who sat in prison under two dictatorships, and you caused one of them. The right side of this house – and no one can neglect that – removed democracy from here, and that was you and your predecessors, the Christian Social Party... For your information, you threw the left side of the house out of Parliament."

In 1984, the fiftieth anniversary of February 1934 showed to what extent the scars still hurt and how deep some of the old feelings run. Intended as a commemoration in the spirit of reconciliation, it was blemished somewhat by a historical debate about "divided guilt." Who was more responsible for destroying the First Republic, the zealous Christian Socials or the zealous Social Democrats? This is an important question in Austria because the party most responsible for the tragedy of 1934 is often considered to be most responsible for creating a situation that led right up to the catastrophe of 1938.

Austro-Fascism or Austrian Patriotism?

There is really no consensus among historians about what type of ideology or social order Dollfuss introduced on May 1, 1934, when Parliament – without the Social Democratic representatives, of course, – adopted a new constitution transforming Austria into a "Christian Corporate State." Reflecting either the vagueness of the term fascism or their own political dispositions, historians have coined a number of terms to describe what Dollfuss and his followers represented: Austro-fascism, clerical fascism, a semi-fascist dictatorship, a conservative dictatorship, an authoritarian state, or authoritarian corporatism with some democratic traits. Historians left of center prefer the first three terms; right of center, the latter three. There is one relatively sure method for finding out the political convictions of an Austrian: ask when fascist rule began in Austria. If the answer is 1934, you are dealing with a socialist.

The "Fatherland Front" undoubtedly resembled existing fascist organizations and rituals with its flags, uniforms, marches, rallies, youth organizations, and the like, and Dollfuss' ideology had a number of affinities with the Nazism of his archenemy Hitler as well as the fascism of his friend and supporter Mussolini: a one-party system under authoritarian leadership, a corporate model of society, and anti-Marxism. Dollfuss even had detention camps established for his opponents, one of them in Wöllersdorf some thirty miles south of Vienna. Although he imitated many features of fascist ideologies, Dollfuss never had the power exercised by the *Führer* or *il Duce*, nor did he, for that matter, ever enjoy the same degree of popular support. Furthermore, central features of fascism like imperialism, racism, anti-semitism, or anti-clericalism were never part and parcel of Dollfuss' ideology, nor can the treatment of his political prisoners in Wöllersdorf be equated with the fate of inmates in Dachau, the first Nazi concentration camp which Hitler established in 1933.

Dollfuss' biggest problem was that by winning the "war" with the Social Democrats, he lost the people. His own base of power was narrow and consisted of a conglomeration of different interest groups ranging from conservatives and clerics to the *Heimwehr* and industrialists, the petty bourgeoisie, and farmers. With the Austrianism of his ideology, he merely alienated Austrians with German leanings and with his "fascism," the socialist segments of the population. He was caught between the passive resistance of the Social Democrats, who had polled 41 % of the votes in the elections of 1930, and the agitation of the illegal Nazi Party which was constantly gaining ground on the right. One thing both of his opponents had in common was that they despised the Austria Dollfuss represented, although for different reasons.

Dollfuss never had a chance to realize his political plans. On July 25, 1934, he was killed in the Federal Chancellor's Office in Vienna during an attempted putsch by Austrian Nazis. It took the government five days to eliminate the various nests of Nazi resistance throughout Austria, and when the fighting was over there were over 200 dead and 400 wounded divided between the two sides. The Austrian Nazis had obviously overestimated their own strength and underestimated the Austrian will to resist.

Dollfuss' legacy is ambivalent. The Dollfuss regime provided the only substantial armed resistance that National Socialism met in Europe before World War II broke out, and some conservatives see Dollfuss as an Austrian patriot who promoted the idea of Austrian independence and hence was the forerunner of today's Austrian national consciousness. However, his critics are quick to point out that he was a fascist responsible for undermining democracy in Austria and presiding over the bloodbath of February 1934, and they sometimes maintain that a democratic Austria could have resisted Hitler in 1938. Conservatives counter that the Social Democrats consistently undermined the idea of Austrian independence by propagating an Anschluss with a democratic Germany. The list of conjectures and counter-conjectures could go on and on.

The heart of the matter is that the conservatives proved they could not solve Austria's problems alone. For a balanced appraisal of the merits and shortcomings of both camps, one has to consult a "non-partisan" observer like the Austrian communist Ernst Fischer: "The Austrian tragedy... was that the democrats were not patriotically Austrian enough and the Austrian patriots were not democratic enough, that the patriots did not believe enough in the democratic strengths of the people and the democrats did not believe enough in Austria."

6. The Nazi Intermezzo

Kurt von Schuschnigg, Dollfuss' successor, assumed a precarious political inheritance. His domestic power base was narrow, and after fascist Italy signed the "Axis Agreement" with Nazi Germany in 1936, Austria lost its only real ally. The "Fatherland Front" failed to unite pro-Austrian and anti-Nazi forces in the country because it was impossible for the Social Democrats to support Austria if it meant supporting a regime they considered fascist. Austria was also diplomatically isolated. This status was a result of historically strained relations with its immediate neighbors and partially a reflection of Western European democracies' disapproval of the turn events had taken in Austria starting in February 1934.

Under these circumstances, Austria faced Nazi Germany alone, and Hitler used a combination of economic reprisals and political threats to erode the position of the Schuschnigg regime. Schuschnigg attempted to resolve Austrian-German differences on a diplomatic level, but Hitler used a negotiation strategy which he would successfully reapply elsewhere in the future: he rewarded his partner's concessions with categorical guarantees that proved to be worthless. Realizing how desperate the Austrian situation had become, Schuschnigg decided in March 1938 to ask the Austrian people directly if they wanted independence from Germany in order to prove to Hitler and the world that an Anschluss was out of the question. He planned to hold a plebiscite to that effect on March 13, 1938, but this merely provoked Hitler into action.

The Anschluss

Even though it fit into his long-range strategy, Hitler's move to occupy Austria was a snap decision. On March 11, 1938, Schuschnigg was told that if he did not resign and allow the formation of a Nazi government under the chancellorship of Arthur Seyss-Inquart,

Hitler's speech on Heldenplatz in Vienna on March 15, 1938.

a National Socialist minister who was the product of one of his previous concessions to Hitler, Germany would invade Austria. Hitler gave the German Eighth Army orders to prepare for "Operation Otto." (These plans for the invasion of Austria had been named after a completely different eventuality, the possibility of a restoration of Habsburg rule in Austria by Otto, the eldest son of the last Austrian emperor, Karl, who had died in exile in 1922.) Resistance appeared futile to Schuschnigg, who did not want to assume the responsibility for spilling blood that he thought would not change the course of events, and he resigned after a moving speech that ended with the phrase: "God protect Austria!"

Seyss-Inquart formed a short-lived Nazi government, and at 5 a. m. on the morning of March 12, leading Nazi security and SS officials flew into Vienna to start taking things into their own hands. At 5:30 a. m., the first German troops crossed into Austria, but the operation was so poorly prepared that a fair number of German military vehicles had to stop at Austrian gas stations for fuel which drivers either confiscated or paid for in German *Reichsmark,* the future currency in Austria.

Hitler joined the columns of the German Eighth Army, visiting his birthplace in Braunau am Inn in Upper Austria and the province's capital of Linz, where he had spent part of his youth. The jubilant reception he received convinced him that his gamble had paid off, and he decided to annex Austria outright.

On March 15, 1938, Hitler gave a speech in Vienna from the balcony of the *Neue Hofburg,* a wing of the Habsburgs' former imperial residence, and some 200,000 Viennese collected on the *Heldenplatz* below to hear him seal the fate of Austria. Nazis called Austria the *Ostmark,* a reference to the borderland role it had played as part of Charlemagne's "German" empire in the 9th century, and Hitler festively reinaugurated Austria's role as a bulwark when he proclaimed the country's disappearance from the map of Europe: "The oldest eastern province of the German people shall be, from this point on, the newest bastion of the German Reich."

The overwhelmingly positive response that German troops received in Austria as well as the optical impression Hitler's *Heldenplatz* spectacle left behind certainly helped convince the world that the Anschluss was merely a matter of Germans dealing with "Germans." These events are the basis of Austria's most negative and sinister cliché: Austria, a country full of Nazis.

There were many reasons for the warm welcome Hitler received in Austria. First of all, Austrians considered themselves Germans in a broad sense of the word and an Anschluss was something that each of the political camps had supported in one form or another at some time. Hitler was a charismatic leader. For some people, the *Führer* and the *Reich* undoubtedly were psychological substitutes for the loss of the emperor and the empire in 1918. For others, they represented the resolution of the intolerable domestic tensions that had plagued Austria since its inception. There were a fair number of Austrian Nazis and their sympathizers as well.

It is important to distinguish among these groups in terms of their relative sizes and different motivations. The largest group undoubtedly consisted of those people who had some kind of pro-German leanings, followed by people who were fascinated by the entire *Führer* cult. The Nazis, the smallest group, can be divided into two subgroups: a larger one, the opportunists or fellow-travellers who had just joined the party as a matter of self-interest or circumspection, and a smaller one, the "old warriors" or "illegals" who had joined the party as a matter of conviction before 1938 — an estimated 120,000. By 1942, there were some 600,000 Nazi party members in what had been Austria, but it would be inaccurate to assume that all of these people were hardcore Nazis. The fact that the percentage of Austrians who joined the Nazi Party was, proportionately speaking, higher than in Germany is more an indication of opportunism or the force of circumstances than dedication.

When looking back at these events, it is also important to differentiate between the pre- and post-war image of Hitler. Very few Austrians or politicians in Western democracies anticipated either the war or Auschwitz. In 1938, Hitler was a controversial but frequently respected politician, and he could look back on a considerable list of accomplishments which offset the distasteful aspects of his ideology for some people. He had pulled the German economy together, reduced unemployment with social public works projects like the construction of the *Autobahn,* and reinstilled the German people with a feeling of self-respect. With a mixture of criticism and a matter of fact recognition of his achievements, the January 2, 1939 issue of *Time* magazine designated Hitler "Man of the Year '38." (The *Time* award should not be misinterpreted as an editorial sign of approval, but it did testify to the magnitude of Hitler's achievements – as dubious as they may have been – as well as his role as a newsmaker. Stalin received it in 1939.)

There are any number of conjectures about what could have happened if Schuschnigg had decided to resist, but the will to resist was not sufficiently present in Austria, nor among Western democracies for that matter. The Anschluss was a gross violation of the World War I peace treaties with Germany and Austria and international law, but the only countries to lodge protests were Chile, China, Mexico, and the USSR. Nowadays historians agree that the majority of Austrians would have voted *Ja* for Austria had the Schuschnigg plebiscite been held, but this is only a hypothetical consolation.

The Nazis recognized the necessity of legitimizing the Anschluss after the fact, and they set up their own plebiscite scheduled for April 10, 1938 to do so. Some of the most important organizational work they did involved rounding up their political opponents and putting them in "protective custody." During March and April alone, over 20,000 Austrians were arrested, and on April 1, 1938, the first trans-

TIME

THE WEEKLY NEWSMAGAZINE

MAN OF 1938

From the unholy organist, a hymn of hate.
(Foreign News)

Hitler, "Man of the Year," 1938: "From the unholy organist, a hymn of hate."

port of 151 Austrians left Vienna for Dachau. It consisted of prominent Jewish businessmen, intellectuals, and leading figures from across the political spectrum. Seven years later, some of the survivors would reassume important positions in Austrian public life. Among them were two supporters of the Schuschnigg regime, Leopold Figl and

Alfons Gorbach, future conservative chancellors of Austria's Second Republic.

The propaganda leading up to the Nazi plebiscite was well orchestrated and had two main thrusts. On the one hand, it was organized around a slogan of national unity: *Ein Volk, ein Reich, ein Führer*, and on the other, it was social or even socialistic. The Nazis attempted to portray themselves as allies of the Austrian working class who had freed Social Democrats from the oppression of the Christian Corporate State. As a sign of solidarity, the Nazis demonstratively burned down the detention camp Dollfuss had founded for his opponents in Wöllersdorf. They tried to convince the working class to abandon its "international, Jewish, and Marxist" socialism for the sake of a national, Aryan, and German one, and the accomplishments of the Reich were supposed to illustrate what the right kind of socialism could achieve. The Nazis also introduced a number of effective relief and employment programs, and it is really hard to tell how many rank-and-file socialists lost their sense of political orientation in this situation. For members of the Fatherland Front and *Heimwehr*, parallels between "Austro-fascism" and National Socialism inevitably facilitated a number of conversions.

On April 10, 1938, 99.7% of the Austrians voted *Ja* for the Anschluss, a result which, if not critically interpreted, merely reinforces the *Heldenplatz* impression. This election was hardly free and democratic. In Vienna, for example, 18% of the eligible voters were excluded from voting for racial or political reasons. Very few people really believed that the ballots were secret, and at some election offices people were "encouraged" not to use the voting booths or simply told what to do. Nazi terror and propaganda created fears and illusions which, paired with the hopes and convictions of some Austrians, produced an optimal result that can only be matched by the "free and democratic" elections held in communist countries today.

Integration and Collaboration

Austria literally disappeared with the Anschluss. In the *Ostmark*, as Austria was called, the Nazis even banned the word Austria, which necessitated changing the names of the provinces of Upper and Lower Austria to Upper and Lower Danube *(Donau)*, and in 1942, the *Ostmark* was renamed the Danube and Alpine Reich's Provinces. These nominal changes merely reflected Nazi policy towards Austria. They wanted to remove each and every reminder of Austria's former independence or unity.

The Nazis' propaganda of national unification actually obscured some of the other important reasons behind the Anschluss. Austria provided Germany with a large reservoir of economic and military manpower. The Anschluss increased the population of the Reich by about 7 million or 8.5%, and over one million Austrians served in German uniform during World War II. It also enlarged the Jewish population of the Reich by 40% — the great majority of Austria's some 180,000 Jews were Viennese— therefore adding a new dimension to the "Jewish problem."

The Nazis were also interested in Austrian natural resources and industry, the militarily vital branches of iron ore, oil, and steel production and processing in particular. The great majority of Austrian banks and companies came under German title, and tremendous investments were made in armament related industries. New steel works, for example, were erected in Linz and named after one of Hitler's main advisors, Field Marshal Hermann Göring, the commander of the German air force.

The Ostmark was strategically important, too. Historically the gate to the Balkans, it served as a springboard for the German invasion of Yugoslavia in 1941. However, in 1938, it was the prerequisite for solving the so-called "Sudeten question." There was a minority of 3 million Germans living in Czechoslovakia along the borders of the Reich which Hitler wanted to "bring home" like the Austrians. The Chechoslovak government asked the British and French prime ministers to negotiate with Hitler on its behalf, and Chamberlain and Daladier agreed to allow Hitler to annex these German-speaking territories in September 1938. Chamberlain spoke of maintaining "peace in our time," but this concession was merely a prelude to the Nazi dismemberment and partial occupation of Czechoslovakia six months later.

The only Germans Hitler did not "bring home into the Reich" in the process of amending the post-World War I borders of Central Europe were the German-speaking South Tyroleans. This exception was a concession Hitler made to Mussolini for allowing him a free hand in Austria. Once the war began, South Tyroleans were given the so-called "option:" the choice between denying their German heritage and language in the form of "Italianization" or "relocation" in

117

territories occupied by Nazi Germany which had a geographical resemblance to South Tyrol, like the Carpathian Mountains.

There was also much talk about the "southeastern mission" of the *Ostmark* which was supposed to become a trade and manufacturing center and exploit the resources and markets on the Balkan Peninsula. Vienna was envisioned as a Hamburg of the southeast. However, given the fact that Germans had a virtual monopoly on the important decision-making positions, the *Ostmark* became part of the Reich's political and economic hinterland. Any economic prosperity in the *Ostmark* was of the most illusory sort. It was related to the war.

Some Austrian Nazis hoped that their branch of the party would maintain some independence or that they would assume leading positions within the administration of the *Ostmark*, but neither of these expectations was fulfilled. The Nazis strictly subordinated the Austrian branch of the party to Berlin and filled many of the leading administrative positions in the *Ostmark* with Germans. Part of the Nazi policy of integrating Austria into the Reich involved introducing laws, administrative structures, and organizations that conformed to those in Germany. Bureaucrats and other civil servants, the police, and the army were absorbed into the various organizations of the Reich, and in some cases people were reassigned to new tasks elsewhere. The Germans did not want to leave the administration of the *Ostmark* solely up to Austrians and had to provide for them after they had been displaced by Germans.

Joseph Bürckel from Hesse, for example, replaced Seyss-Inquart, who later became responsible for the Nazi adminstration of Holland, a task he pursued with such zeal that he was executed as a war criminal after the Nuremburg Trials in 1946. Nazis of Austrian origin were also overrepresented in the occupied territories of Czechoslovakia, Poland, and Yugoslavia. One reason for this apparently was that the Germans assumed that Austrians — and the Viennese in particular — had a special knack for working with foreign peoples which was part of their multinational historical experience. There may also have been a certain propensity to place Austrians in less prestigious posts outside of the Reich. One of the results of these practices was that Nazis of Austrian origin were disproportionately overrepresented in those areas where the atrocities of the "final solution" where committed. Simon Wiesenthal, head of the Jewish Documentation Center in Vienna, estimates that Nazis of Austrian origin were in positions of responsibility related to the deaths of over 3 million Jews.

In the occupied territories, Germans of Austrian origin had two strikingly different reputations. On the one hand, they distinguished themselves from the Germans from the Reich by demonstrating proverbial Austrian traits. The average soldier seemed to be more easygoing, lax, or willing to make exceptions than his German counterpart. On the other hand, some Austrians were much more ruthless than the Germans from the Reich. An unusually large percentage of Nazi war criminals of Austrian orgin had last names which betrayed their families' non-German heritages. In many cases, their grandfathers had been 19th century Czech immigrants to Austria, Vienna in particular. Products of multinational assimilation, they were frightening examples of Austrians who had completely abandoned the tolerance of the Old-Austrian idea by embracing the principles of a peculiarly Austrian form of German nationalism: German superiority and anti-semitism. Denying their heritage, they tried to be more German than the Germans. This type of overcompensation based on humble origins or feelings of inadequacy undoubtedly existed among some of those Austrians with German backgrounds also, and it merely reinforced their commitment to the Nazi ideology.

In a legal or technical sense, it is actually inaccurate to talk about Austria during World War II because there was neither an Austrian state nor an Austrian government. This situation makes it problematic to speak of Austria's political or collective responsibility for the war; however, one can speak of Austrians' responsibilities in terms of their individual contributions to the Nazi war effort.

For anyone whose historical experience is limited to the civil rights one exercises in a functioning democracy, it is hard to imagine the terror that the Nazi system generated. The pressure to cooperate and conform was enormous and the consequences of not doing so draconian. A lack of commitment was immediately suspicious, and small acts of opposition like publicly criticizing the regime, listening to an enemy radio station, or even telling political jokes were crimes of "treason" that were severely punished. The average soldier from Austria followed orders, just as the people on the home front supported the war effort. The nature of the Nazi regime and the demands of the war really did not appear to give the average man or woman, who was interested in survival instead of heroism, many other choices, and the Austrians were, after all, Germans.

119

Persecution and Resistance: Becoming Austrian

In 1918, Austria lost an empire, but it maintained its imperially diverse cultural heritage to a great extent; in 1938, Austria became part of an empire which systematically attempted to destroy Austria's multinational and multi-ethnic heritage. The Nazis' perverted conception of German culture did not tolerate the foreign or so-called non-Aryan influences which were essential characteristics of the Old-Austrian tradition, and the Nazis intended ideologically and physically to purge Austria of its non-German elements.

Right after the Anschluss, the Nazis' immediate concern was rounding up their ideological opponents, but zealous members of the Nazi rank-and-file thought the "Jewish question" was most important. The Anschluss unleashed the full anti-semitic potential latent in Austria; Nazis and their sympathizers forced Jews to scrub streets or otherwise humiliated and maltreated them in spontaneous pogroms. Under the pretext of making confiscations, Nazi officials or people pretending to be the same—bullying and an armband with a swastika were legitimation enough in the days immediately after the Anschluss — plundered Jewish property and possessions. The party hierarchy tried to stop these excesses but merely because they were self-aggrandizing. The Nazis wanted to exploit the Jews systematically and channel anti-semitic sentiments.

It is an incontestable matter of fact that anti-semitism in Austria was worse than it was in Germany itself, partially because it was a more pronounced part of Austria's political traditions. However, this attribute does not necessarily imply a widespread commitment to Nazi ideology, or, as one laconic saying goes: "The Austrians were not very good Nazis, but they were good anti-semites."

Shortly after the Anschluss, the Nazis organized official campaigns aimed at excluding Jews from public life and financially ruining them. They curtailed Jews' civil rights, organized boycotts of Jewish businesses, and saw to it that Jewish civil servants or private employees were dismissed.

The immediate response of many Austrians, whom the Nazis obviously would not tolerate for political or racial reasons, was to flee, but leaving the country was no simple matter. One had to have the appropriate documents and money, and on April 1, 1938, Switzerland, Czechoslovakia, and Hungary made visas mandatory for Austrians in order to protect themselves from a flood of unwanted

In Vienna, the Anschluss was accompanied by an outburst of anti-semitism. Some Jews were humiliated by being forced to paint anti-semitic slogans or the Star of David on Jewish-owned businesses or buildings: an Orthodox Jew carrying a can of paint in his right hand (l.); a young Nazi with a swastika armband on his left arm (r.).

refugees. Nevertheless, thousands of Austrians illegally fled the country and took the risk of being caught on either side of the border. Unsuccessful attempts to flee illegally frequently ended in Nazi prisons or concentration camps.

Many of those who had neither the courage nor the means to flee despaired. Between March and May 1938, 203 Viennese Jews committed suicide; during the same time span the year before nineteen Jews had taken their own lives.

In 1938, the Nazis' strategy for answering the "Jewish question" involved discrimination and terror coupled with "Aryanization" and emigration. The purpose of Aryanization was systematically to relieve Jews of their money, property, and other assets before allowing them to emigrate, and in August 1938, the Nazis established the Central Office for Jewish Emigration in Vienna in order to speed up the process. (One of its most enterprising officers was a Nazi from Upper Austria who later assumed responsibility for the mass transport of Jews from all over Europe to the death camps, Adolf Eichmann.) In addition to answering the "Jewish question," these policies provided spoils for the Nazis. In Vienna alone, Nazi "commissioners" took over some 25,000 Jewish businesses, and the Nazis redistributed some 70,000 flats which had been vacated by Jews who had emigrated or, later, were deported to concentration camps.

The Jews bore the brunt of Nazi terror in Austria. However, they were relatively fortunate in comparison to many of their other European counterparts. The Nazi emigration policy allowed approximately two-thirds of them to escape the Holocaust: the fate of some 65,000 Austrian Jews. Once the war started, emigration became increasingly difficult, and this opportunity disappeared altogether in 1942 when the Nazis adopted the policy of the "final solution."

Around 130,000 Austrians managed to flee after the Anschluss and the great majority of these emigrants were Jews. It would be hard to imagine what the intellectual landscape of the Anglo-American world in particular would look like today without the contributions of these Austrians who fled. Sigmund Freud and his daughter, Anna, emigrated to London, and by chasing Freud and his disciples out of the Reich, the Nazis contributed to spreading psychoanalysis all over the world. The operetta composer, Oscar Straus, and one of the fathers of modern music, Arnold Schönberg, fled to the United States, and Hollywood became a center of émigré authors, artists, and composers. Lise Meitner, a Jewish physicist who developed the theory of atomic fission, worked in Vienna and Berlin before fleeing to Sweden, and other Austrian physicists participated in the Los Alamos Project, the construction of the atomic bomb, in the USA. Philosophers like Karl Popper and Rudolf Carnap debated with each other in Vienna before their ways parted. Popper emigrated to New Zealand, and later to England, where he became globally renowned. Carnap went to the USA to become one of the most important 20th century American philosophers. Conductors like Bruno Walter and Georg Szell left Vienna for careers in New York and Cleveland. There are innumerable examples of this kind of violently induced cultural cross-fertilization, an "Austriafication" of the world.

Emigration, Aryanization, and the "final solution" represent an irrevocable loss for Austria, and they drastically changed the complexion of Austrian culture not only from 1938 until 1945, but also permanently. After the war, Austria failed to make a concerted effort to repatriate those who had fled, and many emigrants were no longer interested in returning to Austria because they remembered well how they had been maltreated. As a result, the Nazis' racial purge of Austria made *homo alpinus* the more typical Austrian after 1945. As paradoxical as it may seem, the birth of the Neo-Austrian idea during the Anschluss period was concomitant with the destruction or flight of many representatives of Old-Austrian culture, and both of these phenomena contributed to provincializing the Austrian idea altogether. The Anschluss marks a cultural hiatus in Austrian history which, in many respects, is more incisive than the year 1918. When the Nazis Aryanized Austria, essential elements of Old-Austrian cultural traditions — like a multi-ethnic heritage or the cosmopolitan touch of the assimilated Jew — disappeared almost completely.

Among the Austrians who fled, however, there was a small group of exiles who had every intention of returning to Austria. These politically active individuals attempted to organize Austrians in exile, but the Allies never recognized any one of the various organizations of political exiles as the legitimate representative of the Austrian people. Spread out all over the world and ideologically disunited, these groups never really stopped quarrelling among themselves and continued to relive and refight the old ideological battles of the First Republic. (Otto von Habsburg, incidentally, was in the United States where he negotiated with the State Department about establishing an "Austrian Legion," but his aspirations, most likely part of a restoration plan, were to no avail.)

Within Austria, however, the Nazis provided Austrians with a common enemy, and political persecution contributed to the resolution of old political conflicts. As Kurt Skalnik, an Austrian journalist and historian, once remarked: 'The switch for Austria's future was thrown in the concentration camps of the Third Reich. Impressed by

123

their common fate, the imprisoned representatives of the parties, which had fought a civil war with each other in 1934, quickly agreed not to work against each other in the future, but together."

Propagated as an act of German national unification, the Anschluss actually reinforced some of the traditional biases cultivated by many Austrians and Germans. They merely had to be reformulated in new terms. Even though there was just one German *Volk*, the Austrians referred to the Germans in terms of the *Alt-Reich*, the "old Reich," as opposed to the "new" Greater German Reich Hitler proclaimed in March 1938. The Germans, on the other hand, frequently spoke of the former Austrians as *Ostmärker*. The *Ostmärker* stereotypically accused the Germans from the *Alt-Reich* of being pedantic, arrogant, and condescending, and the Germans, in turn, criticized the typically Austrian traits of the *Ostmärker* who were considered to be slovenly, indecisive, and ingratiating. A widespread feeling among the residents of the *Ostmark* was that they were discriminated against because of their origins or treated as second-class Germans. This sentiment contributed in a negative sort of way to the development of an Austrian national consciousness.

Hitler also did not keep his promise to the Austrian people. He guaranteed them peace and prosperity in 1938 and gave them war and austerity after 1939. It is one of those quirks of history that many Austrians only discovered for themselves what it meant to be Austrian after they had become German. In their attempt to destroy the idea of Austria, the Nazis actually killed the Anschluss idea for most Austrians and created the preconditions for the development of an Austrian national consciousness which was neither nostalgically Old-Austrian nor pro-German but rather Neo-Austrian: an affirmation of Austrian national particularity, independence, and smallness.

As positive as they may have been initially, Austrians' attitudes towards the Anschluss, Hitler, and National Socialism deteriorated in the course of the war. Hardships produced dissatisfaction, and after the Battle of Stalingrad ended in January 1943, it became increasingly clear to most Austrians how the war was going to end. These are only pragmatic reasons for changes in attitude, but more and more Austrians also came to recognize the full implications of National Socialism. A spirit of opposition developed which spanned a broad spectrum of motives ranging from commonplace resentment to political idealism.

There were a great number of Austrians who had been enthu-

An inmate from the Nazi concentration camp of Mauthausen in Upper Austria who committed suicide by running into the high-voltage fence surrounding the camp; in the background, barracks.

125

siastic Germans in 1938, but became committed Austrians — Austrian in a new and an unprecedentedly nationalistic sense of the word — by 1945. The majority of Austrians experienced a genuine national and, in some cases, political change of heart in the course of World War II.

Within this context, however, it is important to distinguish between attitudes of opposition and the activity of resistance. Many Austrians developed the former, and very few participated in the latter. For a variety of motives, there was active resistance to National Socialism in Austria across the political spectrum from the very start — ranging from Catholic nuns and priests to Moscow-oriented communists — but the resistance movements were small. Resistance should not be exclusively identified with daring acts of sabotage and guerilla warfare; it was conspiratorial and dangerous, but frequently without any real military significance. As in most other occupied territories, conformism was the rule and resistance was the exception, and there were a number of conditions which made resistance more difficult in Austria than elsewhere.

The cultural, ethnic, and linguistic differences between Austrians and Germans were minimal, and Austria was part of the Reich. This made conspiratorial work exceedingly difficult, and the various Austrian resistance groups did not manage to coordinate their operations until 1944 when they founded the Provisional Austrian National Committee. Austrian resistance received very little help from outside the country until towards the end of the war, and the Allies had no real appreciation of it.

Resistance also was an extremely dangerous activity for select idealists who were prepared to risk their lives knowing that their actions were of negligible strategic or military importance. However, resistance was morally and politically important because it provided a series of crystalization points for the ideals of freedom and independence.

The Nazis dealt ruthlessly with all forms of opposition and arrested some 100,000 Austrians between 1938 and 1945 for political reasons. It is fair to assume that the 34,000 Austrians who died in the concentration camps and prisons of the Third Reich or were executed after trials were engaged in resistance, and an estimated 100,000 Austrians were directly involved in resistance movements at the end of the war. Given the circumstances of Austrian resistance, these figures are noteworthy, but it would be inappropriate to exaggerate either the size or military importance of the movements. Austrian resistance does not overshadow the *Heldenplatz* cliché, but it corrects it to a certain extent.

The Reich's Air-Raid Shelter

By the beginning of World War II, most of the world had recognized the Anschluss as a matter of fact, and the war itself merely reinforced a tendency among the Allies not to distinguish between Austria and Germany. As a result, many western democracies interned Austrian refugees along with Germans as citizens of a belligerent power when the war began, and they only gradually began to differentiate between ex-Austrians and Germans. One of the tragic consequences of this policy — combined with the self-serving immigration restrictions imposed by many countries — was that it allowed the Nazis to catch up with tens of thousands of emigrants and exiles from the Reich in 1940 when they invaded France, Europe's traditional haven of asylum.

In the course of the war, however, Allied diplomats and strategists rediscovered Austria. At a conference in Moscow in the fall of 1943, the foreign ministers of the UK, USSR, and USA issued a brief declaration that marked the beginning of a joint Allied policy towards Austria. The "Moscow Declaration" called Austria "the first free country to fall victim to Hitlerite aggression," and stated that the Allies wished "to see re-established a free and independent Austria," but it closed with an admonishment: "Austria is reminded, however, that she has a responsibility which she cannot evade for participation in the war on the side of Hitlerite Germany, and that in the final settlement account will inevitably be taken of her own contribution to her liberation."

The wording of the declaration was ambiguous and led to a number of problems later. It spoke, for example, of Austria when there was neither an Austrian state nor an Austrian government, and it defined Austria as a victim and as an accomplice of Nazi Germany at the same time. However, it did affirm the Allies' intention to re-establish Austria, which was the most important point for the time being. (Austrians in exile were completely out of touch with the situation at home, and some socialists in exile considered maintaining the Anschluss after the defeat of Nazi Germany, a patriotic shortcoming

127

Bombs away! An official US Air Force photograph taken during a raid on Graz's train station and rail connections on April 2, 1945; upper left hand corner: Graz's historical center with the "Schlossberg."

conservatives seldom fail to mention.) The Allies' motives for wanting to re-establish Austria actually had nothing to do with Austrian national aspirations to independence. For the Allies, Austria was merely a peripheral question related to the treatment of Germany, and the re-establishment of Austria, an idea which fortunately coincided with the desires of most Austrians, was primarily a measure aimed at weakening post-war Germany.

As long as there was a war to be won, the Allies made no strategic distinctions between the treatment of Austria and Germany because Austria was fully integrated into the Reich, and Austria played a key role in the Nazi war effort. During the first half of the war, Austria could not be reached by Allied bombers operating from British airfields. Therefore, the Nazis transferred more and more strategically important industries from the *Alt-Reich* to the Danube and Alpine Reich's Provinces which were nicknamed the "Reich's air-raid shelter."

The Allied invasion of Northern Africa and Italy marked the end of this illusory sense of security because it allowed the Allies to establish airfields that brought Austria into range. The Allies virtually controlled the air by August 13, 1943 when the first American air-raid in Austria was flown on Wiener Neustadt, a city of 40,000 thirty miles south of Vienna which was one of Germany's most important aircraft manufacturing centers. After that, air-raid warnings, daily pilgrimages of mothers with their children to air-raid shelters, and bombing became regular events. Throughout Austria, the Allies bombed cities with industrial potential or important rail connections from twenty to fifty times. The German anti-aircraft batteries actually could do very little to stop the destruction. They managed to shoot down fewer than 1% of the attacking planes, and after the Battle of Stalingrad ended in January 1943, the anti-aircraft batteries were manned predominantly by sixteen- and seventeen-year-old boys because all able-bodied men had to be transferred to duty on the front.

Over 35,000 people in Austria were killed in air-raids, some 75,000 apartments throughout the country were fully destroyed and 100,000 heavily damaged. By the end of the war, Austrian industry and transportation were in shambles along with a series of historical monuments. Even though there were fewer civilian losses and not as much sheer physical destruction in Austria as in Germany, these facts were of little consolation to the people who had lost families or emerged from bomb shelters to find familiar surroundings a pile of smoking ruins.

The Nazis' response to Allied bombings was to put their most important projects underground. For example, they manufactured the He-162, the world's first jet-propelled fighter, in a gigantic natural cavern in Hinterbrühl near Vienna, but it never was produced on a large scale. Projects elsewhere in Austria showed how the Nazi war industry throughout the Reich depended on concentration camps to compensate for the labor power displaced by military service. Inmates from Mauthausen, a concentration camp in Upper Austria where over 100,000 people of various nationalities, religious beliefs, and political convictions were murdered during the war, provided slave labor for a number of important projects through a network of forty-nine sub-camps. (Dachau also had thirteen sub-camps in western Austria.) For example, the Nazis used forced labor to dig huge tunnels into the Alps to provide bomb-proof shelters for important projects like the construction of "wonder weapons." Parts of the V-2 rocket testing and manufacture program were located in Upper Austria.

By the beginning of 1944, it was clear to the Nazis that the Reich would have to be defended on the ground, and in the course of that year, 80,000 people — inmates from concentration camps, forced foreign laborers, Hungarian Jews, and members of Nazi youth organizations — began work on the "Southeastern Wall," part of the "Reich's Defensive Line" along the Hungarian border. Scraping the bottom of the barrel, the Nazis mobilized last reserves by drafting all able-bodied men between the ages of sixteen and sixty into the Volkssturm (People's Assault). But by the time the front reached the Austrian-Hungarian border in March 1945, the German Army was so decimated and disorganized that the trenchworks of the "Southeastern Wall" and reserves of the Volkssturm made no difference at all.

7. Allied Occupation:
Four Elephants in a Rowboat

It would be an exaggeration to call the battles fought on Austrian soil at the end of World War II decisive. By the time Soviet troops reached the southeastern border of the Reich at the end of March 1945, the Red Army in the north was just forty miles from Berlin and the Western Allies had already crossed the Rhine. The invasion of Austria was part of a subordinate strategy of forcing Nazi Germany to its knees.

Soviet soldiers on Vienna's Ringstraße firing mortars during the Battle of Vienna in April 1945.

The heaviest fighting in Austria took place in the East. The Nazis declared that Vienna was to be held at all costs — a fate it was fortunately spared — and on April 3, 1945, the Red Army launched a major offensive and took most of the city within ten days. By the end of the war on May 8, 1945, the Soviets had taken Burgenland and the eastern half of Lower Austria, about one-sixth of the country. Some Soviet soldiers conducted themselves in a manner which merely confirmed the gruesome prophecies of Nazi propaganda: plundering, murdering, and raping. (It is interesting to note that the excesses of the Red Army are remembered by Austrians much better than the fact that over 20,000 Soviet soldiers died in the process of freeing Austria from Nazi rule. Given the post-war experience with the Soviets in Eastern Europe, it is of course difficult to imagine them "liberating" anyone. Nonetheless, many Austrians do not show an adequate appreciation of the Soviet sacrifices, just as many Western Europeans or North Americans do not sufficiently recognize how important the Red Army was in terms of winning the war in Europe.)

A major concern among the Allies in the West was the assumption that the Nazis had created an "Alpine Fortress," a series of fortifications in the impassable Alps which could drag the war on indefinitely and postpone Nazi Germany's unconditional surrender. As it turned out, the "Alpine Fortress" was a figment of military imagination blown completely out of proportion by Allied fears.

The disintegration of the German front in the West at the beginning of May facilitated the advance of Allied troops, which met only sporadic resistance in western Austria. The US Third Army reached the border of Upper Austria on April 30, 1945, the day Hitler committed suicide in his Berlin bunker, and fanned out into the province. Shortly thereafter, the US Seventh Army marched into Salzburg and Tyrol. In Innsbruck, Austrian resistance fighters under the leadership of Karl Gruber, the future foreign minister of Austria who later became Austria's ambassador to the United States, gained control of the city just before American troops arrived. The Americans, who were perplexed to see the city decorated in red-white-red flags and a bit suspicious of the warm welcome they received, refused to accept Innsbruck from its local liberators and demanded that a German officer be found who would formally capitulate.

The French invaded Vorarlberg and western Tyrol, a task executed with the help of two Moroccan divisions, and British troops from northern Italy reached the Italian-Carinthian border on May 7, the

Cleaning away rubble in Bregenz, the provincial capital of Vorarlberg, after the war.

day before the war in Europe ended. Then they marched into Klagenfurt where they met units of Tito's partisan army. The presence of the partisans struck fear deep into the hearts of the Carinthians, for whom the Carinthian-Yugoslav border conflict of 1918 was a relatively fresh memory.

Southern Carinthia, an area which had been contested by Yugoslavia after World War I, and parts of Styria were the only areas in Austria where larger scale partisan fighting took place during the war, and the partisans operating there were predominantly Slovenes or communists supported by Tito. The Nazis and the partisans dealt ruthlessly with each other as well as with the civilian population which was subject to punishment by both sides. Neither the Nazis nor the partisans hesitated to shoot or "relocate" civilians whom they suspected of collaborating with the enemy. As a result, some of the bitterest memories and the hardest feelings about the war in Austria can be found in the Carinthian-Styrian borderland where no clear fronts existed. There the populace's sense of allegiance was frequently drawn along ethnic lines, the Slovene "freedom fighters" being regarded as "bandits" by some of the German-speaking population.

The advent of peace in Austria was chaotic. The Allied advances had driven about one million German troops into Austria, along with an array of their comrades-in-arms. For example, there were 150,000 Croats who had fought with Germany against Tito and 50,000 Cossacks who had fought against the Soviets. (In accordance with Allied agreements, both of these groups were "repatriated" after the war, which meant execution or severe punishment for the former in Yugoslavia and almost certain death for the latter in the USSR.) There also were well over half a million civilian displaced persons in Austria, mostly refugees who had fled ahead of the advancing Red Army from all across Central Europe. One of the indigenous civilian population's first reactions to the chaotic conditions was to plunder warehouses where the Germans had stockpiled food because normal chains of distribution had broken down completely.

In spite of extensive planning, the Allies were woefully unprepared to deal with the broad spectrum of problems which confronted them in Austria. Initially each local commander dealt with the situation as he saw fit, which merely led to a multiplicity of standards throughout the country. There was no coordinated policy towards Austria. The country was occupied by four victorious armies, but the formal agreements dealing with the joint Allied occupation and administration of Austria were still in the process of being negotiated at the end of the war (and were not to be signed until the beginning of July 1945).

Founding the Second Republic

The collapse of the Nazi regime and the initial disorganization of the occupational forces created a political vacuum in Austria which allowed Austrian parties and politics to come back to public life. The resistance movements had provided underground contacts for ideological compatriots as well as a pluralistic forum of opinion which spanned the entire political spectrum, and once the front passed through any given province, politicians and parties emerged from the underground ready to accept the challenge of revitalizing Austria. However, the re-establishment of political life was a rather uncoordinated and disjointed process which began on a local or regional level because the lines of communication throughout the country had been torn by war and occupation.

Soon after the Battle of Vienna ended in mid-April 1945, the Soviets were prepared to allow the foundation of "democratic and anti-fascist" parties in their occupied territory. The leaders of the Communist Party of Austria (Kommunistische Partei Österreichs or KPÖ) returned to Vienna from Soviet exile and training in the wake of the Red Army. Representatives of Austria's socialist tradition founded the Socialist Party of Austria (Sozialistische Partei Österreichs or SPÖ) and conservatives founded the Austrian People's Party (Österreichische Volkspartei or ÖVP).

Completely independent of these events, Dr. Karl Renner, the most respected elder statesman in Austria, emerged from retirement to begin an unanticipated and unusual second career. The seventy-four-year-old Renner had retired in Gloggnitz some fifty miles south of Vienna, and when Soviet troops entered the town on April 1st, he went to the local commander to complain about excesses committed by Soviet soldiers. Renner was immediately recognized as a politician of stature, and he was passed up the chain of command. Once at the top, he began high-level negotiations with the Soviets concerning the re-establishment of Austria.

Renner obviously enjoyed the support and the confidence of the Soviets, and on April 20, 1945, the Soviet front commander received orders from Moscow to make Renner responsible for forming a provisional government. This news came as a bit of a surprise to the newly formed political parties in Vienna, which had just agreed upon a provisional mayor for the city, but Renner and the parties' interests were the same. On April 27, 1945, the three existing political parties proclaimed the Second Republic and appointed Renner state chancellor of a provisional government. History practically repeated itself because Renner had assumed a similar position in 1918. In spite of the war and occupation, the preconditions in 1945, however, were in some respects better than they had been in 1918. It was clear to all of the politicians involved that they could not pick up where they had left off in 1934 or 1938, and they recognized that a coordinated effort was the only chance Austria had. The Austrians had suffered through the hardships of Nazi rule and the war together, and they faced the uncertainty of Allied occupation and the enormity of reconstruction together.

However, the proclamation of the Second Republic surprised most people, the Western Allies and western Austrians in particular. Only a fraction of eastern Austria had been liberated by the Soviets when the provisional government was proclaimed. From a Western perspective, the Soviets had allowed and promoted the foundation of a provisional government, although this was a measure which the Allies had neither planned nor agreed upon for Austria. As a sign of circumspection, Renner had also included two communist ministers in his provisional cabinet, and there was a fair amount of suspicion in the West that the whole government was just a communist puppet.

Politicians and political parties in western Austria emerged from the underground later than in the East because the Allied advances there did not occur until the beginning of May. Austrians established provisional town and provincial governments, which the respective Allies supervised and patronized, and then they sought contacts with each other. It was much easier to move within the individual Allied zones than to cross them. Therefore, the provisional federal government and political parties in Vienna had virtually no contact with their provincial counterparts in the West. These difficulties merely aggravated the traditional provincial biases against Vienna, which now appeared to be crawling with communists. Renner's first contacts with politicians in the West were by courier and show how difficult it was to communicate right after the war. At the beginning of May he sent a messenger from Vienna to Tyrol who needed 17 days to complete his journey.

Austria had been re-established — formally at least — but Renner realized that the Austrians outside the Soviet zone had to recognize the provisional government before the Allies would be prepared to do so. Nothing less than the unity of Austria was at stake. In the course of the summer of 1945, informal and, from the Allied point of view, in some cases even illegal contacts between Vienna and the provinces allowed the provisional federal government and the central party organizations to gain credibility in the West. During the same time span, the Allies also finally agreed upon how they were to occupy and administer Austria. Meanwhile, the population suffered all of the consequences of being a war-torn and occupied country, which were magnified by the absence of a nationwide Austrian or Allied administration.

One Divided by Four

The Allied agreements dealing with the occupation and administration of Austria were in many respects similar to the ones made for Germany. The zones and control agreements signed on July 4 and July 9, 1945 divided Austria into four occupational zones which were to be administered along the lines of a jointly formulated policy. France was assigned Vorarlberg and Tyrol; Great Britain, Carinthia and Styria; the USA, Salzburg and Upper Austria south of the Danube; and the USSR, Upper Austria north of the Danube, Lower Austria, and Burgenland. Vienna was subdivided in a similar manner (with the exception of the 1st district of the inner city, which was an international sector alternately administered on a monthly basis by each of the Allies). The Allied Council, the four-power government for Austria, consisted of the Allied High Commissioners (the respec-

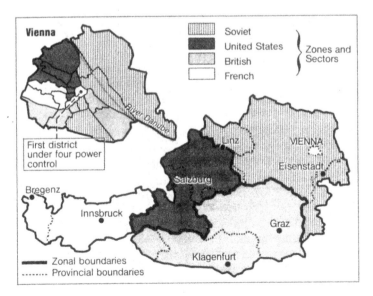

tive zonal commanders) who met in a joint body and were to agree unanimously on policy for the country. The Allies also established the Inter-Allied Command for Vienna, a miniature version of the same arrangement. There were two symbols for the occupation of Austria. One of them was the Allied identification card issued in four languages, an absolute necessity for crossing zonal borders. The other was the special Allied military police force operating in Vienna, the "four in a jeep." One military policeman from each of the occupational powers was assigned to common quadripartite duty on the same jeep.

It took most of the summer for the Western Allies to shift their troops into the assigned occupational zones, transfer contingents to Vienna, and organize their staffs accordingly, and during this period the Western Allies conscientiously ignored the Austrian provisional government. At its first meeting in September 1945, the Allied Council proclaimed itself to be the supreme authority in the country with the objectives of organizing a central administration and democratic elections. Through a series of informal contacts, however, the Western allies convinced themselves of the credibility and integrity of the Renner government. After the provisional government reorganized itself to include members from the Western provinces, thus making it more representative, the Allies recommended that it be formally recognized (well over five months after it had been founded) and mandated it to hold elections in November 1945, the first free and democratic elections in Austria since 1930.

Before the elections, one of the greatest unknowns on the Austrian domestic scene was the strength of the Communist Party. The KPÖ's expectations were commensurate with the other parties' fears, and many observers assumed the KPÖ had the potential of polling about one-third of the votes. However, after the ballots were tallied, it was clear that the KPÖ was not going to play a major role in Austrian politics. In spite of Soviet support — or as some historians maintain, because of it — the KPÖ managed to attract a mere 5% of the voters. Instead of experimenting most Austrians reverted to their interwar electoral preferences. The conservative ÖVP made a strong showing in rural areas and with the middle class, and the socialist SPÖ attracted its traditional urban working-class following, a group which was not prepared to participate in any radical communist schemes.

The political parties formed a coalition government with a conservative chancellor and a socialist vice-chancellor, divided the

138

"Four in a Jeep," a symbol of Allied occupation: (l. to r.) British, American, Soviet, and French military policemen on joint duty in Vienna.

ministerial positions between each other, and symbolically appointed one communist to the post of minister for energy and electrification. This constellation, a coalition of all parties, is reminiscent of how the First Republic began in 1918; however, the domestic politics of the Second Republic developed in a much more auspicious manner. The conservatives and the socialists shared power in a series of coalition governments for over two decades, a partnership which was untouched by the fact that the communists left the coalition in 1947 and slowly sank into the abyss of political insignificance. If confrontation is the key term for an understanding of the First Republic's politics, cooperation was the main characteristic of the Second Republic's initial decades.

The elections in November 1945, the formation of a government, and the first sessions of Parliament in December 1945 were the prerequisites for normalizing Austrian-Allied relations, which seemed to be a rather simple and straightforward matter, in theory at least. The Allied Council was to observe and advise the Austrian government, but it reserved the right to block or send legislation back to Parliament for amendment. In practice, there was one Austrian government but four zones of occupation. Each Allied High Commissioner was also a zonal commander. He could not only block Austrian legislation, if it did not appear to be in his country's interest, but also pursue arbitrary policies in his own occupational zone. Zonal commanders and their troops had the authority to act virtually independently of Austrian federal or provincial authorities.

Two examples suffice to show how this situation complicated reconstruction. Initially, the zonal commanders exercised a peculiar form of provincialism by wanting to keep as many goods as possible in their respective zones. This practice was undoubtedly good public relations, but it was bad economics. It led to a slow and uneven distribution of goods, hindered reconstruction, and actually added impetus to the black market which flourished after the war. Allied aid was also distributed rather unevenly. The Americans and the Britains were more able to give than the French or the Soviets who, on the contrary, were interested in exploiting Austrian resources to repair their own war-torn economies.

A prime example of how Allied policies diverged along the lines of the pending East-West split involved the question of so-called "German assets" in Austria. According to Allied agreement, each of the occupational powers had the right to administer and dispose of German assets in Austria. Distinguishing between pre-1938 Austrian assets and German assets that had been accumulated between 1938 and 1945 was no easy matter, and the Soviets chose to interpret the entire question in a rather broad manner by claiming practically all of the assets in their zone: heavy and light industry, transportation, energy and mineral extraction, etc., a large share of Austria's industrial potential. The Western Allies' response was to turn most of their assets over to the administration of the Austrian government, which had passed a nationalization law for major industries and banks in an attempt to coordinate reconstruction. The Soviets, however, would not allow the nationalization law to be applied in their own zone and continued to do as they pleased, busily dismantling industrial sites for transport back to the USSR (or, in some cases, dismantling them and letting them rust by the wayside). The Soviets even set

"The Big Four" by Ironimus, 1955. The elephants of Allied occupation in the Austrian rowboat.

up a special trade organization for "the Soviet administration of German assets in Austria" called USIA which was simply an organized drain of Austrian economic potential.

Two facets of contemporary Austria's economy still reflect the legacy of occupation. Today Austria has the highest degree of nationalization of any Western European democracy, a trait of its economy which initially had very little to do with the principles of socialist economic planning. Furthermore, the areas of the country which economists call "structurally weak" are most prevelant in those provinces that were previously occupied by the Soviets. Allied occupation added a new and lasting structural dimension to the traditional differences between East and West in Austria. The better political conditions and greater investment in the Western zones of occupation gave them an economic head start on the Soviet-occupied provinces in the East and created a gap which the East has never been really able to close. As a result, many of the previously most underdeveloped Alpine regions of Austria are now the most modern. This change represents an inversion of traditional roles which has merely been reinforced by tourism's commercialization of the Alps.

The political and enonomic burden of Allied occupation was inordinately large for Austria. Karl Renner, elected as the first president of the Second Republic in December 1945, compared Austria's situation to having four elephants in a rowboat. Austria's problem was to get rid of the elephants but salvage the rowboat, a task which appeared to be more and more difficult. The negotiation of the Austrian State Treaty — not a peace treaty but a document designed to regulate Austria's re-entry into the community of nations — started in London in January 1947, but as East-West relations cooled to a chill, it became increasingly clear to the Austrians that they were going to have to live with their elephants for quite some time.

However, in 1946 a new control agreement limited the restrictions the Allies could exercise over the Austrian government, and once Allied-Austrian relations normalized, fraternization became part of everyday life. The Soviets never really managed to overcome the first bad impression they made, and British troops had a reputation for being correct in that distinctively British sort of way. The French use of Moroccan troops from their own colonial empire added an exotic touch to the occupation of Vorarlberg and Tyrol, and they provided for a few unusually dark-skinned Alpine children. Black GIs were a source of constant amazement in the American zones of occupation, the first real experience most Austrians had ever had with *echte Neger,* "real Negroes." Americans are also fondly remembered for distributing bubble gum and chocolate to children in addition to providing Marshall Plan aid. Nevertheless, it would be an exaggeration to be overly sentimental about the cross-cultural contacts of occupation.

Austria's post-war problems were perhaps best captured by a mock version of the Austrian national anthem. Instead of praising the geographical and cultural diversity of the land — mountains, rivers, fields, cathedrals — it began by commenting on the staples of the Austrian diet and the country's political dilemma: "Land of beans, land of peas, occupied by four armies . . . ."

Very few Austrians had the combination of equanimity and optimism demonstrated by the legendary provincial governor of Upper Austria, Heinrich Gleissner. A Soviet officer once indignantly complained to him: "You act as if we were not here at all!" Gleissner responded with a brief history lesson: "Look, Austria has been occupied time and again ever since it has existed: by the Romans, the Swedes, the French, the Germans. They all left, and you will go home, too."

Liberation or Occupation?

The Austrian reaction to the Soviet Red Army's advance into Burgenland at the end of March 1945 cannnot be compared, for example, to the French response to the Allied landing in Normandy in June 1944, even though both of these events signaled the beginning of the end of Nazi rule for each people. By the spring of 1945, the great majority of Austrians viewed the Nazi regime as undesirable and indefensible, but not as foreign, at least not to the same extent it had been foreign for people in other occupied territories. Austrians knew that the end of the war meant the end of Nazi rule, but having been Germans, their desire for liberation was intermingled with the dread of being among the defeated.

A quarter of a million Austrians died in German uniform during the war. After seven years of Nazi propaganda it was difficult suddenly to view yesterday's enemies, the Soviets in particular, as today's friends, and the foreign troops which invaded Austria conducted themselves as victors, not as allies. It was ominously unclear to the Austrians what their future was going to be. Therefore, many people spoke of the end of the war as *der Zusammenbruch*, "the collapse." What had collapsed was the Third Reich; what followed was occupation.

Nowadays, the terminology an Austrian uses to describe the events of 1945 says a lot about his attitudes towards the Nazi interlude. *Zusammenbruch*, which is still common among some members of the older generation, is used in an almost apologetic manner and even can have connotations to the effect that individual aspects of National Socialism may not have been all that bad. *Das Kriegsende*, "the end of the war," or *die Besetzung*, "the occupation," both rather neutral descriptive terms, are probably the most common designations. *Die Befreiung*, "liberation," is problematic because it has so many shades of meaning. Its usage usually reflects a critical historical distance or has the status of a political declaration, and it is more freely and frequently used by the members of those younger generations which did not experience the end of the war. The problem with the term "liberation" is that it does not adequately describe the way the Austrians felt or were treated at the end of the war. Along with arbitrary treatment by the occupiers, hunger, illness, and fear characterized the immediate post-war experience of most Austrians. In light of this, some Austrians made the following ironic observation: "We could survive another war, but not another liberation." Then the Allied occupation of Austria drew on endlessly. Austrians recognized that they had been "liberated," but they were far from being free.

Even though he formally addressed only the citizens of his country on May 8, 1985, the president of the Federal Republic of Germany, Richard von Weizsäcker, actually spoke for all people who had been Germans during the war when he gave a speech commemorating the fortieth anniversary of the end of the war in Europe: "For us Germans, May 8 is not a day of celebration... Some were liberated, while for others it was the start of captivity... Some Germans felt bitterness about their shattered illusions, while others were grateful for the gift of a new start... The feelings of most people were those of exhaustion, despair, and new anxiety. Looking back, they saw the dark abyss of the past and, looking forward, they saw an uncertain dark future. Yet with every day something became clearer, and this must be stated on behalf of all of us today: the 8th of May was a day of liberation. It liberated all of us from the inhumanity and tyranny of the National-Socialist regime."

This speech by von Weizsäcker, unprecedented in its frankness and unmatched by Austrian politicians, was not necessarily popular among the members of his generation, and its central message can be applied to Austria, too. Recognizing the end of the war as a liberation hardly allows qualifications. It is a difficult insight for some members of the generation who were old enough to serve and suffer in the war — about 20% of Austria's current population — because it involves admitting that all their sacrifices were not only in vain but also in the service of an inhumane and criminal regime.

One of the big differences between Austrian and German attitudes involves the fact that the Austrians were freed from a dual yoke: Nazi and *German* rule. The development of an unprecedented Austrian national consciousness and a widespread and deep appreciation for democratic institutions and practices were by-products of the Anschluss, National Socialism, and the war. After having been Germans, Austrians became Austrian; however, after having become Austrian, many people frequently could not understand having been Germans. A similar situation existed with many Austrians' political attitudes. There were any number of Austrians in 1945 who in 1934 had affirmed the end of parliamentary democracy or in 1938 genuinely affirmed the Anschluss. Many of these Austrians became democrats in the course of their experience with Nazi totalitarianism. However, having become democrats made it difficult for some of them to understand not always having been democrats, nor did 1945 appear to be good time to admit previously having been either German or anti-democratic.

The national and political changes of attitude which many Austrians experienced colored their interpretation of their not so distant pasts. Critics are quick to note that the joy of becoming Austrian had a tendency to repress the feelings of guilt which might have accompanied having been German. The peculiarity of the Austrian situation also allowed many Austrians to avoid the type of moral and political soul-searching which was expected of Germans.

The unusual status of the re-established Republic of Austria contributed to a widespread lack of public remorse. The Allies had called Austria "the first victim of Hitlerite aggression" in the Moscow Declaration of 1943 and had made this a cornerstone of their joint policy towards the country. The interpretation of Austria as a victim — a status which corresponded well to the feelings of many Austrians and provided a convenient excuse for some others — was officially and legitimately adopted by the Republic of Austria after the war because it justifiably wanted to be treated like a liberated state instead of a vanquished Nazi colony or ally. Austria had been one of the first victims of Nazi Germany, and it was not interested in assuming collective responsibility for what Nazi Germany or individual Nazis of Austrian origin had done in its absence.

This point may appear to be a lot of legalistic hair-splitting, but there was an important distinction between Austria's status as a state, which did not participate in the war, and Austrians' responsibilities as individuals, who did. As long as the final conditions for Austrian freedom remained negotiable — until 1955 — political circumspection appeared to demand that the entire debate about National Socialism in Austria be held to a minimum. Austria intended to prosecute those Austrians who deserved punishment as Nazi accomplices, but it was not interested in being stigmatized as a former Nazi state because that status would jeopardize favorable Allied treatment altogether.

Nazis, Nazis Everywhere?

During the war, propagandists on both sides used the terms German and Nazi almost synonymously, and the images of those old World War II newsreels are all too vivid. Hollywood then did a good job of refining the Nazi stereotype. The knee-high boots and the broad-billed cap are give-aways which only need to be accented with accessories like a riding crop and a sneer. Given the predominance of the Nazi stereotype, it is actually difficult for some people to imagine what denazification might have been — outside of lining up all those Nazi-Germans or German-Nazis and shooting them. However, most people could not tell you the difference between the uniform of an SS officer who ran a concentration camp, and the one of a normal front officer in the German Army, an army in which one million Austrians served and 250,000 died. Were they all Nazis?

After the war, Austrian politicians and the occupational powers agreed that denazification was a high priority, and it was a particularly pressing issue for Austria because it had to demonstrate to the Allies its own preparedness and decisiveness in dealing with this problem. In 1945, one of the first acts of the Austrian government was to ban the Nazi Party along with any form of "fascist re-activity" and pass a law establishing the prosecution of war criminals. By 1946, 536,000 former Nazis had been officially registered in Austria; that is, any one who had belonged to the Nazi Party or one of its some thirty suborganizations, ranging from the infamous SS to professional and vocational organizations for civil servants, teachers, farmers, or even mothers.

The Austrian government initially dealt firmly with former Nazis. They were excluded from voting and had other civil rights curtailed in addition to being subject to a broad spectrum of penalties. Many "formers" were released from public service or lost their jobs in the private sector, conscripted into work brigades to clean up rubble, had possessions, property, or money confiscated, lost pensions, or were subjected to special taxes. In the decades after the war, Austrian war crime laws provided the basis for 130,000 investigations; 23,000 Austrians were put on trial, and 13,600 found guilty; 43 war criminals were sentenced to death, 30 of whom were executed.

However, denazification raised a number of questions. Politicians recognized the importance and expediency of distinguishing between Nazis who had demonstrated an avid ideological commitment and held influential positions in the Reich, and those low-level party members who had joined organizations either as opportunistic fellow-travellers or out of sheer fear. It also became increasingly clear that an Austrian democracy could not effectively deal with former Nazis by using totalitarian methods like permanently excluding approximately one-sixth of its citizens from participating in the political process without creating a new source of right-wing radicalism. From a more pragmatic point of view, it also was evident that the Austrian economy, which was confronted with the gigantic task of reconstruction, could not indefinitely do without one-sixth of the labor force or permanently demote that group to menial tasks.

As a response to these problems, a new denazification law was passed in 1947 which distinguished between "less incriminated" and "more incriminated" former Nazis. This legislation paved the way for the reintegration of some 500,000 Austrians back into society — in 1948 there was a general amnesty for the "less incriminated" — while upholding the punishments and restrictions upon the 42,000 "more incriminated" who were amnestied for the most part by 1956.

The 1948 amnesty, of course, had a number of political consequences. Both of the major parties, the ÖVP and the SPÖ, were suddenly confronted with the potential of a half a million "new" voters. They both wooed the so-called "formers" and absorbed a fair number of them into their ranks. Some critics maintain that the SPÖ needed the "formers" more than the ÖVP because the socialists' traditional recruitment pools for party managers had been decimated by the exile of leftist intellectuals after 1934 and the destruction of the Jews after 1938. They are quick to point out that the secular and anti-clerical traditions of the socialist SPÖ stood closer to the world-view of most "formers" than the ÖVP's Christian-oriented conservativism and use these premises to explain, for example, how a traditionally "black" province like Carinthia, which had a strong "blue-brown" element, became "red" after the war and has remained so ever since. However, the ÖVP also took many old sheep, which had strayed ideologically in the past, back into its political fold, especially if they

Both the conservative ÖVP and the socialist SPÖ absorbed former Nazis into their ranks, and then self-righteously accused each other for doing so. A caricature by Ironimus from 1966 showing the parties hanging out their "dirty wash."

belonged to the party's traditional rural or middle-class constituencies.

The amnesty allowed Austria's third, national-liberal camp to reassume its traditional spot on the political spectrum. Not all of the "formers" were satisfied with the choice between the two major parties, even though membership in the ÖVP or SPÖ offered them the quickest means of reassimilation. National-minded individuals founded the League of Independents *(Verband der Unabhängigen* or *VdU)* which attracted 12% of the votes in the elections of 1949. The League consolidated with another right-wing group, the Freedom Party, in 1956 to form the Freedom Party of Austria, *Freiheitliche Partei Österreichs* or *FPÖ*, which has since filled the slot of the third camp on the Austrian political spectrum. The FPÖ intially had a reputation for being a stronghold of old Nazis but gradually developed an older, national wing and a younger, liberal one. Winning between 5 and 10% of the votes in national elections in the past two decades, the party never has been able to resolve its ideological identity conflict.

The relative success or failure of denazification in Austria is a matter of perspective, and opinions are frequently divided along generational lines or between political idealists and pragmatists. Younger or idealistic critics lament that too many Austrians conveniently ignore or repress their pasts, or they point out that even though Nazism has been rigorously removed from public life, there is a residue of fascist attitudes in everyday life in terms of some people's feelings towards foreigners, minorities, or Jews. The older generation which lived through the war is quick to reply that everything was not as plain and simple back then as many youngsters would like to believe, and there is no point in tearing open old wounds. Pragmatists frequently mention that the war effectively denazified most Austrians anyhow. They also refer either to the admirable record of Austrian democracy since the end of World War II or to the fact that neo-Nazism in Austria is a marginal phenomenon of negligible importance. In any event, it is striking to notice that many Austrians, who usually demonstrate great pride in their strong sense of tradition and great familiarity with their country's history, are unusually reticent when dealing with the Nazi era.

The entire question of the adequacy of denazification in Austria received a tremendous amount of international attention in 1986. During his campaign for the Austrian presidency, Kurt Waldheim, the former Secretary General of the United Nations from 1972 to 1982, was accused of being a Nazi, a war criminal, or at least a liar. The "Waldheim affair" was extremely complicated; a few points will have to suffice here.

Kurt Waldheim shared the experience of practically an entire generation of Austrian men. He served in the German Army during World War II. There is no conclusive documentary evidence proving he was a member of the Nazi Party or directly involved in atrocities against civilians while he was stationed on the Balkan Peninsula during the war. Circumstantial evidence also seems to be in Waldheim's favor. Waldheim was a low-ranking officer, who did not receive the type of promotions a reliable Nazi could have expected, and it is highly improbable that he was directly involved in atrocities committed by units of the army to which he was attached because he had a desk job as an information officer or translator. Kurt Waldheim, as he once dubiously formulated it, just "did his duty."

However, many people found it incomprehensible that a well-known diplomat running for public office did not provide a comprehensive biography before his campaign began, and in the course of Waldheim's campaign certain details about his past came to light which assumed the status of revelations. His opponents and critics in and outside Austria accused him of trying to embellish his past by falsifying it with omissions, and Waldheim's omissions created the provocative impression he had something to hide, which led to conjectures and accusations. Attempts were made to prove that Waldheim had been a member of the Nazi Party or even a war criminal. Waldheim's critics managed to produce a wealth of documentary evidence about the individual stations of his career as a German officer in Greece and Yugoslavia, but they failed to prove the grave allegations they made. Judging by the findings, Waldheim had nothing to be proud of but also nothing to hide, but he had attempted to hide it nevertheless.

The international attention given to Waldheim's past contributed to obscuring the crux of the "Waldheim affair," which boiled down to being a question of personal and political credibility related to how he dealt with his past. Aside from the initial inaccuracies in his biography, Waldheim made statements about his past in the course of his campaign that did not correspond to documentary evidence to the contrary unearthed in archival research, or, only after such evidence was presented did he admit to things he had previously denied.

Whether Waldheim was forgetful, merely politically inept, or as some of his harshest critics maintained, always one step behind the truth is impossible to ascertain. Granted, it is difficult for anyone to produce a detailed reconstruction of his own past after some forty years, but Waldheim seemed to be peculiarly unacquainted with the stations of his own military career as well as the activities of the army to which he was assigned as an information officer at headquarters. He maintained to know little about the atrocities committed by units of the German Army on the Balkan Peninsula, and nothing about the mass deportation of 40,000 Jews from Saloniki at a time when he was stationed just a few miles away.

For international observers Waldheim's past was the only issue at stake in the presidential election he won in June 1986 with 54% of the popular vote; however, for many Austrians, who naturally viewed their choices from a more differentiated domestic perspective, it was just one of many issues. For example, as the ÖVP-backed candidate, Waldheim appealed to the traditional electoral preferences of many conservative Austrians. His socialist opponent was rather weak and lackluster, and as a conservative, Waldheim also benefited from widespread dissatisfaction with the SPÖ after fifteen years of socialist governments.

The Waldheim affair reached its official denouement in February 1986 when a commission of internationally renowned military historians recruited by the Austrian government to investigate the allegations made against Waldheim submitted its final report. On the one hand, the report cited no evidence supporting the gravest charges made against Waldheim: a previous commitment to Nazi ideology or personal guilt for war crimes; on the other, it accused Waldheim of trying to obscure or trivialize his military past and ascertained that he must have known more about the atrocities committed on the Balkans than he said he did. Some of Waldheim's supporters, who were satisfied with the report's formal exoneration, accused the historians' commission of overstepping its mandate with conjectural conclusions. However, opponents of Waldheim felt that such conclusions were well founded and the most important part of the report. The controversy which ensued contributed more to the polarization of the issue than to its resolution and evolved around the question whether Waldheim's mandate as a democratically elected president had been strengthened or weakened by the report. Supporters argued that his record had been cleared, and opponents demanded his resignation.

Drawing conclusions from the Waldheim affair is not easy. The accusations made against Waldheim— and his own maladroitness— did severe damage to Austria's international image, and there are multitudes of not-so-well informed people all over the world who are probably still convinced Waldheim was a Nazi. It will take Austria quite some time to repair the damage incurred. However, the Waldheim affair did start a debate within Austria and showed how far Austrians are from having established a consensus about how they should deal with the Nazi-German episode of their own history. It illustrated to what extent Austrians disagree on whether or not they have critically come to terms with their past, or conveniently forgotten it.

8. The Second Republic: The State That Everyone Wanted

For years, it appeared to Austrians that the Allied occupation of their country might last indefinitely because the negotiation of the State Treaty, the prerequisite for full independence, stalled as East-West relations deteriorated into the Cold War. Nevertheless, Austria was exceptionally fortunate in the long run. Unlike Germany, which was effectively divided in 1949, Austria did have a freely elected government with a recognized realm of jurisdiction that crossed zonal borders. The Allies, which had formally committed themselves to re-establishing Austria, continued to cooperate there, minimally at least, in spite of the Cold War. In addition to this, neither the Soviets nor the Austrian Communist Party enjoyed enough popular support to let them even begin to consider establishing an "East Austria," and some people argue that Austria simply was too small to divide into two politically and economically viable parts. However, there were some hawks in the United States Department of Defense who thought that it might be a strategically good idea to get on with the Cold War and split the country. Fortunately, the opinions of far-sighted diplomats from the Department of State, who wanted to negotiate a solution, prevailed.

The protracted occupation of Austria was part of the superpowers' Cold War stalemate in Europe, and neither East nor West was willing to change the status quo to their potential disadvantage. One of their concerns was the future military alignment of a fully independent Austrian state. The Soviets looked upon the probability of Austria joining NATO unfavorably, and even though it was clear to the Western Allies that Austria was a functioning Western democracy, the hypothetical possibility of having Soviet troops stationed in Tyrol was equally undesirable. In order to break the Allied stalemate, Austrians began discussing among themselves the idea of permanent neutrality along the lines of the Swiss model. Then they raised it with the occupational powers as an alternative which would dispel mutual fears by giving neither East nor West a strategic advantage.

This proposal – along with the brief "thaw" in East-West relations after the death of Stalin in 1953 – was enough to break the diplomatic ice for the final negotiation of the State Treaty in the spring of 1955. On the one hand, Austria managed to resolve quickly the bilateral questions which were pending with each of the occupational powers, and, on the other, Austria promised to proclaim its own neutrality once the State Treaty had been signed and the Allied occupational forces had left the country; that is, after full Austrian territorial sovereignty had been re-established. On May 15, 1955, the foreign ministers of the signatory powers signed the State Treaty in Vienna's Belvedere Palace, then posed on a balcony with Austrian Foreign Minister Figl, who proudly displayed the treaty to the crowd which had assembled below. On October 26, 1955, the day after the last occupational soldier left Austria – research seems to indicate that he was British – the Austrian Parliament unanimously passed a constitutional law proclaiming permanent Austrian neutrality. Austria was free at last and neutral forever.

The State Treaty, which regulated Austria's official re-enty into the community of nations, contains two articles which are of particular political importance today. One of them, Article 7, addresses the "rights of Slovene and Croat minorities" along the country's southern border. After World War II, Tito's communist Yugoslavia unsuccessfully attempted to revive the old Carinthian-Styrian border issue that had been settled after World War I and aspired to annex a healthy chunk of Austrian territory where Slovene minorities resided: most of Carinthia south of the Drau River and bits and pieces of Styria. Article 7 was a concession made in the course of negotiations to protect the ethnicity and interests of the Slavic minorities there.

It is still relevant today due to the periodic conflicts which arise between Slovenes, who have been guaranteed special minority rights such as bilingual schools, courts, and public offices, and some of the right-wing "national" elements of the borderland population. In the late seventies, for example, there was a heated controversy in southern Carinthia, where some villages have different names in German and Slovene, about the erection of bilingual signs. At a glance, this might seem a bit curious, but it indicates how deep ethnic feelings can run in this borderland. In conflicts of this nature, the Slovenes legitimately refer to their Article 7 rights in the State Treaty.

The Allied foreign ministers and Austrian government officials on the balcony of the Belvedere Palace after signing the State Treaty on May 15, 1955 (l. to r.): Macmillan (UK); (3rd from left) Dulles (USA); Pinay (F); Austrian Foreign Minister Figl holding the State Treaty; Vice-Chancellor Schärf; Molotov, (USSR); and Austria's Federal Chancellor, Raab.

Austria incidentally had its own aspirations to a border revision with Italy after World War II and wanted to rectify the blatant injustice of South Tyrol. In a series of meetings parallel to the Allied negotiation of the Italian Peace Treaty in 1946, the Austrian Foreign Minister, Karl Gruber, and the Italian Minister President, Alcide De Gasperi, drew up the so-called Gruber-De Gasperi Agreement. It did not change the borders, but it did provide South Tyrol with a special autonomy status, the realization of which has periodically been a point of contention between the German-speaking South Tyroleans and the Italian authorities in Rome, as well as Austria and Italy. Opinions differ as to whether or not Gruber negotiated well – most historians agree that, given the circumstances, there were no real chances for a revision – but Tyroleans on both sides of the border were not

154

especially pleased with the results. Some critics maintain that the young, inexperienced Gruber was simply outsmarted by De Gasperi, an elder statesman who also happened to be an Old-Austrian. From 1911 to 1914, De Gasperi was a member of the *Reichsrat*, imperial Austria's multinational parliament, and represented the northern Italian province of Trentino, which at that time was Austrian, not Italian.

The second article of the State Treaty that is especially relevant today, Article 13, imposes a series of bans on special weapons. Since Austrian defense policy is inextricably related to Austrian neutrality, it is perhaps a good idea to look first at just what Austrian neutrality involves.

Austrian Neutrality: Neither East nor West?

If one had to list all the attributes of Switzerland, after watches and chocolates, a fair number of people would mention neutrality, and practically everyone knows that after finishing their active duty Swiss soldiers take their rifles home with them to become part of a reserve militia. On a similar Swedish list, neutrality would perhaps be mentioned after a number of famous exports like Björn Borg, Ingemar Stenmark, and Volvo. On most lists for Austria, it would take a long time to appear, if at all. As an established part of the Swiss and Swedish images, neutrality is supported by political traditions which are well over one-and-a-half centuries old; Austrian neutrality, in comparison, is a novelty which many people do not understand, especially those who think in political terms like "if you are not with us, you are against us."

There are a number of things neutrality is not. It does not mean, for example, that a state cannot take sides on important international issues, nor should it be confused with categorical pacifism. Neutrality principally refers to the manner in which a state chooses to conduct itself when two other states or groups of states are engaged in an armed conflict. By declaring neutrality, a state has the obligation to abstain from the conflict and otherwise treat the belligerents impartially, and it has the right to defend itself if either of the belligerents should violate its territory in the course of hostilities.

Neutrality in the broad sense is an option any non-committed state can exercise in a conflict, while reserving the right to enter future ones. Permanent neutrality as exercised by Switzerland and Austria is the categorical commitment never to enter conflicts. The legal theory of neutrality, which primarily refers to the conduct expected of states in a time of war, also has far-reaching consequences for the political practice of neutral states in times of peace because only the peacetime conduct of a neutral state makes its neutrality credible in case of war.

As a permanently neutral state, for example, Austria obviously cannot join NATO or, a less attractive or plausible option, the Warsaw Pact. Austria also has refrained from making nonmilitary commitments which might jeopardize the credibility of Austrian neutrality by integrating itself into either of Europe's economic blocs: the European Economic Community (Common Market) or COMECON. However, in the late eighties Austria began discussing the possibility of EEC membership with a target date in the early or mid-ninties and engendered a discussion about the compatibility of neutrality with EEC affiliation. A balanced policy of diplomacy and trade always has been part of Austria's practice of neutrality. As one of Austria's most seasoned diplomats, a former foreign minister and the chancellor of a series of socialist governments from 1970 until 1983, Bruno Kreisky, once formulated it, the task of Austria's foreign policy has been "to cultivate in one's friends a maximum of trust, and in the others – because a neutral state really does not have enemies – a minimum of suspicion."

Last of all, neutrality is made credible by the fact that neutral states arm themselves and are prepared to defend their neutrality. However, given the current geopolitical realities in Europe, one has to avoid a number of false assumptions about Austrian neutrality, misconceptions which plague some Austrians themselves. Armed neutrality does not mean that Austria's small army – supported by a reserve militia which is being developed along the lines of the Swiss model – should, in theory, be able to stop a mass attack by the forces of the Warsaw Pact (or, to be fair, NATO) at the border.

On the contrary, Austrian defense policy is based on the scenario that a violation of Austrian neutrality would only be of interest to either of the military pacts if they were fighting a conventional regional conflict and one of them thought they could gain a tactical advantage by using Austria as a land of transit. Austria therefore has developed what it calls a "territorial defense strategy" which is based

"Neutrality" by Ironimus, 1968. Federal Chancellor Josef Klaus representing Austria's position between NATO and the Warsaw Pact.

on defending key zones of North-South and East-West transit in the country. (The strategic paths through Austria have not changed in the last 2,000 years: the Danube Valley, the valleys and passes through the Alps in Tyrol, or the route from Vienna over the Semmering Pass to northern Yugoslavia or Italy.) Austria's defense plans rest on the assumption that the modestly equipped Austrian Army can utilize the advantages of defending a rugged terrain to make the cost of violating Austrian neutrality greater than the potential advantages of doing so. In other words, the advantages of a surprise attack through Austria drop proportionately to the Austrian ability to slow it down. Austrian defense policy is based on deterring invasions in this manner, and the unofficial mascot of the Austrian Army reflects this strategy. The hedgehog is small but it has lots of sharp quills.

However, some Austrian defense experts are concerned about the military credibility of Austrian neutrality, and this is where Article

13 of the State Treaty comes back into the picture. Post-World War II peace treaties and the Austrian State Treaty all have special weapons limitation clauses in them which partially reflect the authorship of the United Kingdom and its experience as an island state during the war. Article 13 forbids Austria from possessing, developing, and experimenting with a number of weapons: torpedoes, submarines, motor torpedo boats, specialized assault craft, and guns with a range of over thirty kilometers (approximately the distance from Calais to Dover). It also prohibits Austria from having any "self-propelled or guided missiles," most likely a reference to weapons like the V-1 and V-2 rockets Nazi Germany unleashed on Britain at the end of the war, as well as atomic or chemical weapons.

As a result of a narrow interpretation of Article 13, Austrian armed forces do not have missiles, which makes them a modern military anomaly, but proponents of defense are pushing for a revision of this policy. Some Austrians are proud of the fact that Austria has not participated in the conventional arms race. They believe that a small non-aligned state like Austria can set a global example for disarmament, and some Austrians were extremely upset in 1985 when the Austrian government finally decided to "upgrade" its airforce by buying twenty-four twenty-year-old, used Swedish Saab "Dragon" jets to replace the thirty completely outdated jets it had. Among the younger generation, a number of people lamented wasting so much money, which could have been productively allocated to environmental, social, or employment projects, on weapons; some military experts accused the government of buying outdated junk. (Switzerland, in comparison, has a modern air force with three hundred machines.)

Not all Austrians fall into these two extreme categories. There are pragmatists who recognize that Austrian neutrality has contributed to European stability. They also realize that Austria has saved a tremendous amount of money by not investing heavily in defense, and they sometimes assume that as a Western democracy the country is implicitly protected from the East by NATO. There are also fatalists, perhaps the typical Austrian, who think that if there is another war in Europe neither neutrality nor missiles will make much difference if the giants clash.

Within Austria there is a noticeable change of attitude towards defense as one goes from East to West. The lowlanders in the wide open spaces of the East, which have been invaded so many times throughout the ages, seem resigned to their fate, come what may; in the more impassable West, however, there is a long tradition of citizens' militia called *Schützen* which in Tyrol, for example, goes back to a 16th century charter by Emperor Maximilian. With their colorful native dress and antiquated muzzle-loading rifles, the *Schützen* nowadays provide a colorful, folkloric background for parades and other festivities, but they nevertheless still symbolize an Alpine will to resist outside aggression.

This brief sketch of some of the more problematic aspects of Austrian neutrality should not overshadow its many positive aspects. In 1918, the last minister president of imperial Old-Austria, Heinrich Lammasch, envisioned neutrality as the most appropriate status for the newly founded Republic of Austria, and he thought a neutral Austria could best contribute to peace and security within the new European order. This idea seemed unusual then, but it is wholeheartedly supported by Austrians now. Austria has perceived its role as a neutral state in terms of active neutrality, and it frequently contributes to the maintenance of peace and security by offering its good services as a nonpartisan mediator or host.

For example, Austria has repeatedly provided asylum for refugees from Eastern Europe: 180,000 Hungarians after the Hungarian Revolution in 1956, some 130,000 Czechoslovaks after Warsaw Pact troops forcibly ended the "Prague Spring" in 1968, and over 40,000 Poles during the Solidarity crisis in Poland in the early eighties received asylum in Austria finding a temporary home or, in some cases, a permanent one. Austria has also granted asylum to thousands of other refugees from troubled countries like Uganda, Chile, and Vietnam. These figures in themselves may not seem considerable, but, given the size of the country, they are impressive. In addition to this, Austria has served as a land of transit for over 200,000 Soviet Jews on their way to new lives in Israel or elsewhere. From the "displaced persons" of 1945 to the victims of political, racial, or religious persecution today, Austria has served as a land of asylum for over 1.7 million people.

Austria has also been active in UN peace-keeping operations. Austrian contingents have served on Cyprus since 1964 and on the Golan Hights between Syria and Israel since 1973. Vienna hosts a number of UN agencies which are housed in the Vienna International Centre, a multi-million-dollar complex on the banks of the Danube which was subsidized by the Republic of Austria and the city of Vienna. It is leased to the UN for a yearly rent of one schilling, less than ten cents.

Austria's geographic position and neutral status seem to predestine it to serve as a meeting place for East and West. Aside from spectacular events like the summits between Khrushchev and Kennedy in 1961 and Brezhnev and Carter in 1979, Vienna has hosted the MBFR troop and conventional arms reduction talks between the representatives of NATO and the Warsaw Pact since 1973. Vienna also hosted the third follow-up meeting of to the Helsinki Conference on Security and Cooperation in Europe in 1986–89, and it is a popular site for other international conferences of all sorts as well.

It would be contrived to try to trace a direct lineage from the imperial Old-Austrian idea of multi- or supranationalism to the contemporary Neo-Austrian idea of neutrality in the service of internationalism; however, both of these ideas show a kindred spirit: an aspiration to resolve conflicts or even reconcile opposites for the well-being of a larger whole.

The Politics of Partnerships

There are a great number of explanations for Austria's post-war success. Undoubtedly the 1.6 billion dollars Austria received in various forms of aid after the war — predominantly under the European Recovery Program, better known as the Marshall Plan — combined with plenty of Austrian hard work were just as important as the structural changes made in the economy, like the nationalization of major industries or an astute Austrian policy of management and investment. All of these things combined to produce an "economic miracle" smaller than the West German one but nevertheless something which has provided Austrians with an unprecedented, if modest, amount of material prosperity and security. From another perspective, it would be hard to underestimate the importance of the State Treaty or Austria's neutrality. Another equally important element responsible for the success of the Second Republic is related to how the Austrian perception of domestic politics changed from the interwar period to the post-World War II one.

Even though the conservatives and the socialists retained their traditional followings after World War II, both camps made obvious

A caricature by Ironimus on the post-war coalitions: the conservative ÖVP (l.) and the socialist SPÖ (r.) sharing the seat of power. The divided telephone symbolizes "Proporz," the practice of parity.

changes in their ideologies which facilitated cooperation, and there was a tendency for the parties to converge on certain fundamental issues. The socialists dispensed with much of the rhetorical and conceptual baggage that went along with looking at society in Marxist terms like class struggle, and the conservatives abandoned many of the intolerant or anti-democratic attitudes which had been part and parcel of their previous definition of "Christian" politics. In other words, both parties affirmed the pluralistic nature of a democratic society, rejected the idea of one-sided radical experiments, and came to respect their opponent's point of view.

It would be a gross exaggeration to call the series of ÖVP-SPÖ coalition governments from 1947 to 1966 a happy marriage, but it was a tolerable one. The parties not only went out of their way to compromise in the daily give-and-take of parliamentary politics; they also agreed to check and balance each other's influence by sharing power through *Proporz*, the proportion or parity system.

In order to understand the theory of *Proporz*, one has to imagine the entire sphere of political influence in society as a checkerboard with black and red squares in the first line, an alternating sequence of red and black squares in the second line, and so forth. The end result, regardless of which direction one moves on the political checkerboard — up, down, or sideways — is an alternating red-black or black-red sequence. In order to complete the picture of the political practice of *Proporz*, one simply has to imagine that certain black squares have been traded for certain red ones, or vice versa. This does not affect the total number of squares each color has at its disposal, but it does create some inordinately large blocks of one color and the other. For example, the ÖVP dominated a traditionally conservative field like agriculture just as the SPÖ controlled a traditionally socialist sphere of interest like labor. (Austrians with a feeling for historical precedents compared *Proporz* to the "dualism" of the Austro-Hungarian Empire. The conservatives had one *Reichshälfte*, "half of the empire," and the socialists had the other.)

All of these changes naturally affected the average Austrian's perception of politics. The combative "us-versus-them" attitude of the interwar period was replaced by a "they-for-us" attitude: "they" – the political parties, bureaucrats, experts, and the like – assuming the responsibility for agreeing upon what is good for "us," the people. Instead of looking at politics in terms of combative polarization, Austrians began looking at it in terms of benevolent stratification, and this point of view was reinforced by the conduct of the political parties and the coalitions.

The more socialists and conservatives abandoned ideological arguments and dedicated themselves to solving concrete problems, the less important politics seemed to be. After all, both the socialists and the conservatives maintained to represent the best interests of *all* Austrians: a catch-all slogan which had become part of each of their new images.

One of the obvious consequences of these changed perspectives was a drop in the average Austrian's subjective sense of "belonging" to a party or believing in the necessity of political engagement. If party membership in the First Republic was a commitment to participate, then in the less heated ideological atmosphere of the Second Republic it has become in many cases a formality or a means of opportunism.

There is a special term used in Austria to designate the abuses inherent in the coalition or *Proporz* system: *Parteibuchwirtschaft*, party-membership-economy. Since the influence of the political parties

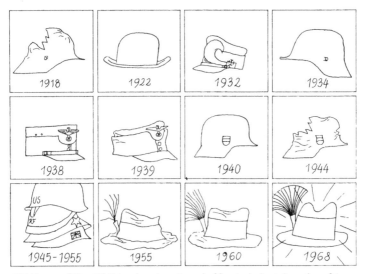

"50 Years of Our Life": Ironimus' portrayal of five turbulent decades of Austrian history using the headware symbolic for each period.

permeates so many spheres of public life in Austria, there is still an open practice of patronizing one's own that goes back to the coalitions. A party membership will open some doors but definitely close others, or, to use the checkerboard metaphor, one can take advantage of the red squares or the black squares, but not both. For example, jobs in the large public and nationalized sectors of the economy or publicly subsidized housing may be distributed upon the basis of "color," party membership, instead of using objective nonpartisan criteria like qualifications or need.

This practice is aggravated by the density of political organization in Austria, a structural carry-over from the "us-versus-them" days of the interwar period. Each of the major parties has well over one million members. The SPÖ, for example, is approximately the same size as its political counterpart in the Federal Republic of Germany, the Socialist Party of Germany or SPD. The big difference, however, is that Austria has about one-eighth the population of the Federal Republic of Germany. After World War II, many Austrians may have stopped believing in political ideologies, but they continued to believe in political parties, even though their reasons for doing so actually damaged the credibility of the parties themselves.

The cruel course of the 20th century has also persuaded more than a few Austrians to view politics with scepticism. After all, there are retired civil servants still around who took five different oaths of allegiance in the course of less than thirty years: to the emperor before 1918 and the First Republic thereafter; to Dollfuss' Christian Corporate State in 1934 and Hitler and his German Reich in 1938; then to the Second Republic in 1945, which was occupied by four different powers representing two opposing ideologies until 1955. Changes as frequent and radical as these do not exactly instill people with confidence in politics.

Consequently, there appears to be a high degree of tolerance in Austria for the abuse of public office: mismanagement, patronage (called *Freunderlwirtschaft* or friends' economy), cover-ups, and the like. Public expectations that politicians have to conform to certain generally recognized moral standards, the violation of which, for example, has forced British ministers out of office in the wake of sex scandals or caused an American president to resign after Watergate, do not seem to be as high in Austria as they are in the Anglo-American world. Some Austrians have the vague feeling that people in high public office nowadays — regardless of their personal integrity and dedication — most likely could not have gotten there without connections and at least a few shady deals, or that one of the trappings of power is the privilege to "arrange" things for political or personal friends.

The relatively low level of political involvement that many Austrians show is not merely a matter of disillusionment. Among some members of the older generations, it can be explained in terms of the historical insight that politics is somehow transitory. They have seen empires and states, ideologies and parties, come and go. Paradoxically other Austrians' lack of political involvement may also reflect favorably upon the success of the Second Republic. It is an indication of how few concerns many Austrians think they have.

The Austrian Way

The series of ÖVP-SPÖ coalition governments started in 1947 and ended in 1966. The ÖVP ruled alone until 1970, and then a thirteen year marathon of socialist governments under the chancellorship of Bruno Kreisky began, which ended in 1983 with a political novelty: a socialist-liberal, SPÖ-FPÖ coalition. In spite of these various transitions, a high degree of consensus has remained one of the characteristics of how decisions are made in Austria. A prime example of this high-consensus, low-conflict decision-making process is a product of the coalition era. It is not a political but an economic coalition called social partnership.

Social partnership is a peculiarly Austrian way of solving problems. Austria's "social partners" are the highest ranking representatives of four different umbrella organizations which represent various economic interest groups: the conservative dominated Chamber of Agriculture and Chamber of Commerce, which also represents private industry in the broadest sense, and the socialist-oriented Chamber of Labor and Austrian Trade Union Federation. In spite of the obvious dovetailing of interests with the respective parties, the social partners regularly meet, independently of the political parties and voluntarily under the nominal auspices of government representatives, to discuss issues of common concern like wages, prices, and economic and social policy. In high level negotiations, the social partners attempt to settle disputes before they become controversies and agree upon terms acceptable to all parties.

The success of this practice, which has been called "class struggle at the conference table," is based on the preparedness of the social partners to compromise, as well as the willingness of the various sub-organizations represented by each of the social partners to accept the results of decisions made at the top level for entire sectors of the economy. For example, if one of the lead unions like the steel workers negotiates a 4% raise in wages, this sets the standard for others. The rail workers will not go out and demand 12%.

Aside from holding down the price-wages spiral, one of the most frequently cited benefits of social partnership is the practical absence of strikes in Austria. For example, at the end of the seventies, an average of two minutes per year were spent on strike for each member of the Austrian labor force. In the Federal Republic of Germany it was 28 minutes; in the United States, 194; in the United Kingdom, 321; and in Italy, 590. These figures show one way in which social partnership contributes to an atmosphere Austrians call "social peace." However, the key to understanding social partnership is not the intricacy of its organization but the underlying attitudes which make it possible. Social partnership is not just an Austrian institution; it is an Austrian state of mind.

Given practices like social partnership, it is easier to understand why Pope Paul VI called Austria an "island of the blessed" in 1971, a compliment which undoubtedly referred more to Austria's social peace, economic prosperity, social welfare institutions, and political climate than it did to the spirituality of its residents. Nevertheless, at that time many Austrians were flattered by the papal praise, and they recognized that the opportune development of Austria was indeed a blessing, a literal one for conservative Catholics and a figurative one for the more sceptical socialists who were in power and just beginning to embark on what came to be called the "Austrian way."

After the boom years of the sixties, Austria mastered the economic turbulence of the seventies with admirable results. At a time when most other countries of the industrialized world were suffering from low growth rates, high unemployment, high inflation, and currency fluctuations, Austria adopted an economic policy based heavily on subsidies and intervention which allowed it to enjoy comparatively high growth rates and maintain low unemployment while keeping inflation down and the schilling stable. The socialists simultaneously managed to increase the density of the meshwork of Austria's "social net," as the sum total of the country's various social welfare programs are called. This constellation of facts helps explain why the quality of life in Austria was rated fourth in the world in a University of Pennsylvania study in the early eighties. The only countries ahead of Austria were Sweden, Denmark, and Norway, and many countries with higher standards of living rated much further down the line.

In the eighties, however, Austrians began to repeat Pope Paul's famous "island of the blessed" phrase with an increasing amount of self-irony and criticism. Austria is not as insular as some Austrians might like to think, nor have Austria's temporal blessings proved to be immutable. Looking ahead, many Austrians sense that the future is not going to be a matter of repeating the successes of the sixties and seventies, but rather a question of maintaining what has been achieved or modestly augmenting it.

More pessimistic critics go as far as to say that the expenditures Austria has made to maintain its prosperity and social peace have been made at the expense of the country's future, and they do not hesitate to make gloomy predictions. They also think that Austria's post-World War II tradition of high-consensus, low-risk decision-making, which has been one of the keys to Austrian success, may turn out to be a deficit in the future because it is too ponderous and inflexible. In other words, Austria has a tendency to minimize its risks. Its economic viability and well-being in the future may depend on learning how to maximize them.

One of the country's problems after three prosperous decades is that Austrian politicians are as unaccustomed to making unpopular decisions as the Austrian people are to accepting or supporting them. Furthermore, if Austria's political parties cannot agree on the terms of sharing responsibility, they have shown a tendency in the past to shy away from assuming it on their own, or they seem to avoid the risk of making decisions which are indispensable for the future but appear unnecessary or unpopular for the time being. Two examples, Austria's nationalized steel industry and its policy towards nuclear energy, suffice to illustrate these points.

During the seventies, the SPÖ was in the double-bind of representing management— because the party was in power and responsible for overseeing the operations of nationalized industry — and labor, their traditional constituency, at a time when the demands of management and labor conflicted. The steel industry drastically needed restructuring, partially at the expense of labor but for the benefit of the industry's future as a whole. However, the SPÖ hesitated to ask its own supporters to make sacrifices because the party had not required concessions from its rank-and-file following for quite some time. The economy was in relatively good shape and cuts in a key industry during a period of growth appeared incongruent with the socialists' own political priorities of job security and low unemployment. Therefore, they postponed the inevitable by tinkering around with small-scale reorganization and pumping enormous subsidies into unviable operations. The ÖVP criticized these measures, but it did not present an alternative acceptable to the socialists. The end result was that by the mid-eighties even some socialists started talking about releasing up to 10,000 employees. The money lost by subsidizing the wrong operations could have been reinvested elsewhere to really secure other jobs.

The evolution of Austria's policy towards nuclear energy provides perhaps an even better bipartisan example. In the late sixties, an ÖVP government decided to build a nuclear generator west of

Vienna in Zwentendorf. The SPÖ assumed this project after coming to power in the seventies. However, by the time the plant had been completed at great expense, environmental and safety concerns had tainted the popularity of the project with the public. Even though the SPÖ had a majority in Parliament and could have opened the plant on its own, it turned to the ÖVP for support arguing that the conservatives had started the project in the first place and, after all, both industry and labor needed cheaper domestic energy in order to maintain prosperity and secure jobs.

Sensitive to the increasingly controversial nature of nuclear energy in general and the Zwentendorf site in particular — it is only twenty-five miles from Vienna — the ÖVP accused the SPÖ of not being willing to assume sole and full responsibility for opening Zwentendorf. In order to avoid this accusation, the socialists came up with the idea of outmaneuvering the ÖVP by "asking the people" and planned to hold a plebiscite which they expected to win. The ÖVP, in turn, encouraged its supporters to vote against Zwentendorf because the socialists were not willing to assume the responsibility for a project the ÖVP had initially started. The entire issue was, of couse, much more complicated than this. However, the conduct of the political parties contributed to aggravating the environmental and safety issues which made the population uneasy, and, as it turned out, the SPÖ lost its gamble 49.5 to 50.5%. The generator never went into operation; it was ironically christened Austria's "atomic museum."

The purpose of this example is not to imply that Austrians have an ecological consciousness which is more highly developed than elsewhere. It merely demonstrates how the two major parties could not agree upon a controversial issue and, in the final analysis, both tried to shirk responsibility. As a result, Austria is the only industrialized country in the world with a complete nuclear generating facility but no nuclear-generated energy, but it covers part of its needs by importing nuclear-generated electricity from the Federal Republic of Germany. (Zwentendorf remained a smouldering issue until the Chernobyl catastrophe in 1986 which overnight turned what many Austrians considered an embarassing political fiasco into a far-sighted environmental decision.) Austria undoubtedly is going to be confronted with other controversial decisions in the future, but it will hardly be able to afford to make them in the manner described above.

Looking Back into the Future

Austrians frequently look at themselves in historical terms, therefore, when they look ahead, they inevitably take a glance back to find historical precedents or examples which can serve as points of reference for the future. The two key political experiences of contemporary Austria have been the catastrophic civil war in February 1934, which marked the beginning of the end of the First Republic, and the post-World War II coalitions which laid the foundations for the success of the Second Republic. February 1934 is solely a negative point of reference. No one is interested in re-creating the hostile kind of atmosphere that prevailed in the First Republic. The post-war coalitions have a dual reputation. For people who look back at the immediate post-war period as a nostalgically transfigured time of collective need and common aspirations, joint ventures and mutual successes, the coalitions represent the we-are-all-in-this-together spirit which enabled Austria to master an apparently hopeless situation. However, the end of the coalition era in the mid-sixties evokes predominantly negative associations: the high-handed and self-aggrandizing party politics of *Proporz*, protection, and party-membership economics.

This is not the place to make a prognosis about Austria's future, but the Austrian elections in November 1986 provided a few indicators about how Austrians see their alternatives. A fair number of Austrians have become increasingly dissatisfied with the political options the established parties represent, and they have become increasingly concerned about environmental issues. Austria's "Green" movement was born in the late seventies during the conflict over the Zwentendorf atomic reactor, and it came into its own in a lowland forest on the shores of the Danube near Hainburg, south of Vienna, where, in 1984, it helped block the beginning of a huge hydro-electric project. In 1986, the Greens, despite factional infighting, attracted 5% of the votes and assumed eight of the 183 seats in Austria's Parliament. Their political advent not only added a new color to Austria's political spectrum; it signaled how far the deterioration of Austria's three traditional political "camps" has progressed, and it marked the end of the two-and-a-half party system. The Greens took votes away from both major parties and, in all probability, have made an absolute majority for either of them a thing of Austria's political past. From now on, Austria will be ruled by coalitions.

169

The liberal-national Freedom Party, FPÖ, also did well in the elections by attracting 10% of the votes and increasing its seats in the Parliament from twelve to eighteen. Under the leadership of a new, young, and dynamic chairman, Jörg Haider, the FPÖ took votes away from the socialists in their strongholds in the East and did the same to the conservatives in theirs in the West. A political chameleon, Haider has the good looks of a ski instructor, is exceptionally effective with the media, a liberal with liberals, and national with nationalists. He knows how to articulate the frustrations of the "little man," and he is a ruthless critic of the major parties' shortcomings. Some observers immediately interpreted the FPÖ's success as a "jump to the right" in Austria. This diagnosis may be a bit alarmist and premature. The success of the FPÖ, however, was clearly an indication of how dissatisfied some Austrians are with the major parties.

In 1986, the socialists lost big, but they still managed to come out of the election as the strongest single party with eighty seats in Parliament. The conservatives lost less, but with their seventy-seven seats they failed to achieve their goal of becoming Austria's strongest party. Ambivalently looking back on the blessings and curses of the old ÖVP-SPÖ coalitions, the leaders of the major parties decided to try to rejuvenate the good and dispense with the bad by forming a new SPÖ-ÖVP coalition. However, some critics fear the concessions necessary to hold the SPÖ-ÖVP coalition together will merely cement high-consensus, low-risk policy-making and produce half-baked solutions to Austria's problems. Others think that the remnants of the old red-black camp mentality may lame the parties' ability to cooperate. More optimistic observers believe that both parties have recognized the necessity of unpopular, high-risk policy and are prepared to assume responsibility for it together.

The old, post-World War II coalitions were a product of conviction and necessity, whereas the new mid-eighties coalition has been more a product of necessity than conviction. This difference is of crucial importance. Nevertheless, Austrians are trying to make a virtue of necessity, and they hope that necessity will also be the proverbial mother of invention.

Postscript: Typically Austrian

This book may end on a much too somber or foreboding note – which is merely a good indication that its author is a foreigner, not an Austrian. It would be typically Austrian to say "the situation is hopeless but not serious," a phrase that goes back to the days when the Habsburg Empire was irrevocably lost but simply refused to collapse. Neo-Austrians repeat this phrase with great relish today because their ironic sense of fatalism still far outweighs any inclination to morbid gravity: a Germanic trait which just makes life more difficult than it already is. However, there is a certain danger in this typically Austrian attitude. For example, if a situation is serious but not yet hopeless, ironic light-heartedness merely allows it to get worse.

Foreigners frequently do not differentiate enough when they use the term Austrian. Calling a particular provincial trait "typically Austrian" is always problematic because it elevates the provincially particular to the status of nationally universal. In other words, portraying one province as typically Austrian inevitably offends the residents of Austria's eight other provinces.

Austrians themselves carefully differentiate between what they do and do not have in common, between provincial or political traditions which separate them and national ones which form mutual bonds. For example, the phrase "typically Viennese" may have positive connotations in Vienna. In the provinces it inevitably has critical undertones and refers to the megalomania of the federal capital's residents. Western Austrians, who make their living entertaining foreign guests, tend to agree that the Viennese are the worst of all foreigners.

In spite of regional rivalries and biases, Austrians do have a sense of belonging together. They have developed a feeling for being a nation, but they seldom show a pronounced sense of nationalism. The Nazis stigmatized the words in the German language one needs to be patriotic. Expressions like *Vaterland* (fatherland) or even *Heimat* (homeland) are still imbued with negative connotations, but

171

these terminological taboos cannot sufficiently explain the Austrians' lack of an affirmative form of patriotism.

Austrian national pride does exist, but it is constantly undermined by other typically Austrian attitudes: self-irony and scepticism. Austrians look at their small state and say to themselves *Wer sind wir in der Welt?* ("Who are we in the world?") This type of statement reflects a dangerous phenomenon called *Kantondenken,* "canton-thinking," or *Verschweizerung:* the "Swissification" of Austria. Calvinism is completely foreign to Austrians, therefore they will never be as self-righteous — nor as successful — as the Swiss. However, Austrians who lose contact with the broader perspectives of the Austrian idea tend to develop narrow, self-complacent attitudes which can be negatively circumscribed as Swiss or geocentrically "Alpine." The best way for a foreigner to evoke an expression of Austrian patriotism is to treat Austria with the same irony and scepticism Austrians exercise themselves. Then they suddenly say: *Wir sind wer...* ("We are somebody...") Austrian patriotism is not a boisterous expression of pride, but an act of self-defense.

Austrians also view the role their country plays in Europe from different perspectives. Sharing borders with three communist states, it appears to some people to be in the East. After all, Vienna is farther east than Berlin, Prague, or Zagreb. However, its economic and political organization place it firmly in the West with other European democracies. As a neutral state it is not a member of either of the military blocs — NATO here or the Warsaw Pact there — so in this respect it is neither East nor West. For pessimists, it has degenerated to a borderland or become a precariously situated and hardly defensible bulwark. For optimists it is a land of peaceful transit, not only for tourists, trains, or freight trucks but also for ideas. A place where East and West meet geographically and politically, Austria has reassumed its old function as the heart of Europe under completely new circumstances.

Austrians are well aware of how large Austria once was and how small it now is. Therefore, they have developed a dual perspective for viewing the relative size and importance of Austria. They have absolutely no illusions about their country's lack of political clout and have accepted its role as a mini-power, but they are practically overcome with feelings of grandeur when they look at Austria's cultural and historical heritage – Austria, the superpower.

Austria has reconciled itself with its imperial past. After 1918, there

*An example of the imperial metaphor: "It was very nice, I was very pleased,"
a famous saying of Emperor Francis Joseph put into the mouth of the socialist
Federal Chancellor and "red monarch" Bruno Kreisky by Ironimus in 1979.*

were very few democrats in Central Europe who could look back
favorably on the Habsburg Empire, and the First Republic con-
sciously tried to dissociate itself from all things imperial. However,
since 1945 the Second Republic has profiled itself as the curator and
interpreter of Old-Austria's imperial cultural heritage. In other words,
the further the political reality of the Habsburgs has receded into the
past, the easier it has become for Austrians to take pride in once having been great. Vienna regards itself as the imaginary capital of a
cultural and intellectual empire which stretches far beyond the former borders of the Habsburg Empire. (Some people in the Central
European states which were formed out of the Habsburg Empire and
are now satellites of the Soviet empire also look back at Old-Austria
with a certain nostalgia. The terms of subjugation then were milder
than they are now, and the idea of Old-Austrian or Central European culture transcends national and ideological borders.)

The use of imperial metaphors would have been unthinkable in

173

interwar Austria, but nowadays Austrians use the term "emperor" to describe the achievements of countrymen who appear to be a degree beyond the superlative. Bruno Kreisky, Federal Chancellor of the socialist governments from 1970 until 1983, received the title "Emperor Bruno" towards the end of his thirteen-year reign. This affectionate and ironic honor was bestowed upon him not just to describe his longevity. Kreisky, a politician of international stature whose reputation and influence radiated far beyond the borders of Austria, was an exceptionally popular and controversial personality. His opponents and critics accused him of developing all the patronizing, paternalistic, and self-righteous habits of a real emperor.

Recently the imperial image of Austria has been rejuvinated and revised. Between 1984 and 1986, gigantic exhibitions on turn-of-the-century Vienna were organized in Venice, Vienna, Paris and New York. An unprecedented fascination with the climax of imperial Austrian culture — "Vienna 1900" — has added a new set of traits to the old Austrian image. Freud, Klimt, and Mahler are providing Emperor Francis Joseph and Johann Strauss with some serious competition.

Critics have accused Austria of using the glory of its imperial past to draw attention away from the less praiseworthy episodes of its more recent history, or they claim Austrians are rather selective in terms of choosing what is typically Austrian. "Beethoven was an Austrian and Hitler was a German" is the most ironically cited example of Austrians' alleged propensity for selective self-definition. However, Austrians are beginning to deal more and more critically with their past, and anyone who understands the Old-Austrian idea realizes that Beethoven and Hitler were both Austrians.

Austrians' reasons for preferring Beethoven over Hitler as an example of what is "typically Austrian" are understandable, but Austrians sometimes have the feeling their critics are set on turning the Nazi cliché into Austria's sole and most representative characteristic. What about mountains-and-music?

Austria does have an international reputation for musical performance and alpine skiing. The Vienna Philharmonic's New Year's Concert, with its light program of polkas, marches, and waltzes and inevitable high point of Strauss' On the Blue Danube, is televised world-wide and has probably the largest global viewing audience of any annual music event. In this respect, it is typically Austrian, but sophisticated music lovers maintain that the Austrian Federal Radio's regular FM broadcasts from Salzburg's annual music festivals are even more typical. This kind of observation makes regular guest performances by Herbert von Karajan and the Berlin Philharmonic typically Austrian.

Austria is also well aware of its contributions to popular culture. Hollywood's most prominent set of muscles belongs to Arnold Schwarzenegger, a body-building Styrian. Falco, a representative of "Austro-rock" whose real name is typically Austrian, Hansi Hölzel, made it to the top of America's pop-and-rock music charts with a hit which was thematically very Austrian, *Amadeus*. Most of Falco's North American fans did not have the vaguest idea he was Austrian, so he gave one of his subsequent songs a tremendously original title to remind them of his origins, *The Sound of Musik*.

Calling "Conan, the Barbarian", or Falco typically Austrian makes highbrow representatives of Austrian culture practically nauseous, and they react the same way when they are exposed to the lowbrow misrepresentation of Austria as a "ski nation." However, if there is one single field of competition in which Austria considers itself a world power, it is alpine skiing. Salzburg's Annemarie Moser-Pröll has been called "the best woman skier in history." Franz Klammer, a farm boy from Carinthia, set an untouchable world record for downhill racing victories in the seventies and subsequently received the title Emperor Franz. In Austria, his popularity is surpassed only by Toni Sailer, the winner of four gold medals at the Winter Olympics in Cortina, Italy in 1956.

When the Austrian ski star, Karl Schranz, was disqualified from participating in the Winter Olympics in Sapporo in 1970 for allegedly having violated his amateur status, Austrian ski fans were indignant. Upon returning to Vienna, Schranz received a hero's welcome, and Bruno Kreisky immediately invited him to report on the disgraceful conduct of the Olympic officals responsible for a great injustice. Tens of thousands of people collected outside the Federal Chancellor's Office demanding to see Schranz until Kreisky appeared with him on a balcony. The dimensions of this outburst of athletically inspired Alpine patriotism were so disturbing for some observers that they drew immediate parallels to the way people had behaved on Heldenplatz in 1938 when Hitler "came home."

Seeking historical precedents and parallels is also typically Austrian. Before the Winter Olympics in Sarajevo in 1984, Austrian sports journalists joked about the bad precedent Francis Ferdinand had set with his showing in 1914. Then the "ski nation" Austria made its worst

175

appearance in decades by winning only one bronze medal. (Nonetheless, Austrian ski manufacturers were pleased with the results because the great majority of victors from other countries skied on Austrian brands — even the American downhill champion, Bill Johnson.)

This book has attempted to illustrate how difficult it is to use a generalization like typically Austrian by showing how multifaceted Austria is. The Austrian usage of the phrase "typically Austrian" probably demonstrates this point better than anything else. When Austrians emphasize something to a foreigner as "typically Austrian," they usually refer to part of their diverse heritage which makes them proud, something beautiful, praiseworthy, or at least quaint. However, when Austrians are muttering among themselves in German, the same phrase, *typisch österreichisch,* is often an expression of criticism, disgust, or even despair.

Appendix:
Typically Provincial — Tips for Touring

Diversity can be overlooked on a small or a large scale. Calling one particular region of an Austrian province "typical" for the rest of that province involves the same kind of mistake one makes by calling one particular province in Austria "typically Austrian." There are, of course, typically Austrian phenomena. Of Austria's nine provinces, only Vienna and Burgenland are excluded from participating in the beauty of the Alps. The Viennese coffee-house can be found in Vienna, of course, but it also is an Austria-wide institution. (Some people maintain that the most genuine "Viennese" coffee-houses are in the provinces.) The custom of vintners' serving their own wine, *Heurigen,* is a typically Austrian institution shared by all wine-growing provinces: Lower Austria, Vienna, Burgenland, and Styria. Nevertheless, each of these phenomena is subject to regional variations which may be dramatic, as they are in the Alps, or more subtle, as they are with coffee-houses and *Heurigen.*

The following sections are illustrations of provincial diversity and, at the same time, suggestions about things to do and see. Each section begins with the names and addresses of the province's tourist information office *(TI)* and provincial museum *(Landesmuseum: LM).* The provincial tourist offices are helpful in providing visitors with information ranging from accommodations to the arts and sports, and they are supported by a network of regional offices. Write in advance outlining your specific interests and needs, and they will provide you with ample information. The museums in each provincial capital have excellent collections on regional history and folklore, and they are a good means of getting acquainted. All of the standard guidebook series – Baedecker, Blue Guide, Fodor, Michelin – have guidebooks on Austria. Which one is the best is perhaps more a matter of taste than anything else. *Austria: A Phaidon Cultural Guide,* edited by Franz Mehling, is an excellent companion for excursions, and it documents the fact that there is hardly a village

177

in Austria without some sort of attraction worth seeing. Last but not least, those people who cannot make up their minds which province or provinces to visit should contact the Austrian National Tourist Office: Österreichische Fremdenverkehrswerbung, Margaretenstrasse 1, A-1040 Vienna. It can provide you with information that will make your choices easier and more difficult at the same time.

Vienna

TI: Wiener Fremdenverkehrsverband, Kinderspitalgasse 5, A-1095 Vienna, tel. (0222) 43 16 08
LM: Historisches Museum der Stadt Wien, Karlsplatz, Vienna

Much to the consternation of many Viennese, Vienna has been called the world's largest open-air museum, but there really is at least one museum for everyone in Vienna. The museums range from morbid (the *Bestattungsmuseum* with its collection on burials and mortuary science) to sobering (the exhibition of the Documentation Archive of Austrian Resistance), from amusing (the Austrian Circus and Clown Museum) to unusual (the International Esperanto Museum), and they cover just about everything in between. There is no reason to point out the obvious like the Imperial Apartments in the Hofburg Palace or the former Habsburg summer residence of Schönbrunn with its beautiful park and one of Europe's oldest zoos. Necrophiles go out of their way to see the coffins of the Habsburgs in the Imperial Vault *(Kaisergruft)* or visit the graves of famous Austrian composers and artists at the Central Cemetery *(Zentralfriedhof)*. Would you like to see where Freud had his couch, where Beethoven lived, where Schubert was born? What about Klimt, Schiele, and Kokoschka in the Upper Belvedere, the former summer residence of Prince Eugene of Savoy which is worth seeing in itself, or the world-famous collection of Bruegels in the Kunsthistorisches Museum? Do you want to see Gothic architecture on a large scale (Saint Stephen's Cathedral), or a small one (Maria am Gestade)? How about Baroque (Karlskirche), or modern ("Most Holy Trinity" in Mauer on the outskirts of Vienna, designed by the sculptor Fritz Wotruba)? Is it better to go the State Opera or catch an operetta at the *Volksoper*? The traditional ball season runs from January 1st until Ash Wednesday, and Vienna holds its annual *Festwochen,* "festival weeks," in May and June. The Viennese coffee-house has to be visited but what to eat? *Sachertorte,* or *Malakofftorte* (to be avoided if you do not like rum, cherries, and whipped cream). What about *Gugelhupf,* a traditionally Viennese marble cake, or *Palatschinken,* normally falsely translated as "pancakes" – actually crepes filled with jam, chocolate, or nuts? Then there is *Kaiserschmarren* which is closer to pancakes but fluffier, richer, and torn into bite-sized pieces before being served with plum preserves seasoned with cinnamon and cloves. The *Heurigen* is also Viennese. Grinzing is quaint but crowded; try Sievering, Stammersdorf, or Mauer for a more genuine atmosphere. There is virtually no end to the choices one has to make. Maybe the best thing to do is to go up to the *Kahlenberg,* a small mountain in the Vienna Woods which overlooks the city and the Danube, and try to get an overview.

Lower Austria

TI: Niederösterreich Information, Heidenschuss 2, Postfach 96, A-1014 Vienna, tel. (0222) 53 33 114
LM: Niederösterreichisches Landesmuseum, Herrengasse 9, Vienna

The historical heart of Austria, Lower Austria, is the country's largest and, in many respects, geographically most diverse province. A tour through Lower Austria begins in Melk with its magnificent Baroque monastery and proceeds down the Danube through the Wachau region, where the river winds through terraced vineyards and orchards. The castle of Aggstein is a well-preserved medieval ruin which gives its visitors a good feeling for what life must have been like in those days. The village of Dürnstein farther downstream, located at the foot of another ruin where Richard the Lionhearted was once held captive, is simply picturesque, as is the historical center of Krems, not far away. The Wachau is dotted with quaint little vintners' villages, and the region is well known for its choice wines as well as an apricot schnaps called *Marillenlikör.* However, as a wine growing area the Wachau also competes with other regions near Vienna as well as south of the city: Gumpoldskirchen, Pfaffstätten, and Vöslau, just to mention a few. *Heurigen* abound in all of these areas. However, Lower Austria is Alpine, too. The Ötscher region is popular for hiking. A ride up the *Schneeberg*, "snow mountain," in an old steam driven locomotive with toothed wheels that fit neatly into slotted tracks in order to make the climb, is a rare opportunity. However, some people prefer the more sedate atmosphere of the spa of Baden with its parks, thermal baths, and annual summer operetta. From there they proceed to Mayerling, a Carmelite convent built on the site of the hunting lodge in which the son of Emperor Francis Joseph, Crown Prince Rudolph, committed suicide with his teenage mistress, Maria Vetsera, in 1889. Heiligenkreuz, a medieval monastery in the Vienna Woods, is the next logical stop, because Maria Vetsera's grave is in the village cemetery. People seeking solitude may go to the *Waldviertel*, "forest-quarter," north of the Wachau, or visit the adjoining *Weinviertel*, "wine-quarter." Each of these regions is typically Lower Austrian. There are a series of art and music festivals held throughout Lower Austria, too. Churches and castles, monasteries and small palaces are the sites of innumerable events often unjustly overshadowed by the happenings in Vienna but frequently providing a worthy alternative to them.

Burgenland

TI: Landesfremdenverkehrsverband für das Burgenland, Schloss Esterházy, A-7000 Eisenstadt, tel. (0 26 82) 33 84

LM: Burgenländisches Landesmuseum, Museumsgasse 1 – 5, Eisenstadt

One of the main attractions of Burgenland is Lake Neusiedl. A traditional center for water sports of all kinds, the large – 124 sq. mile – but shallow "steppe lake" is surrounded by a belt of reeds which provide weaving material for local handicrafts. Fresh fish served from the lake reflect a culinary mixture of Hungarian and Slavic influences and are frequently seasoned with red paprika and garlic. (Incidentally, *Karpfen*, carp, is a game fish and a delicacy in Central Europe.) The area east of the lake, *Seewinkel*, partakes in the atmosphere of the Hungarian Plain, and the rustic villages on the western shore (Rust, Mörbisch) are famous for their quaint atmosphere, off-season at least. Storks which nest annually on the chimneys of the houses in these villages are local ornithological attractions. Along with Kobersdorf, Mörbisch is also one of the sites for Burgenland's annual *Festspiele* (festival) held from the end of May to the end of August. In Mörbisch, operettas are performed on a provisional "lake-stage" which allows the audience to watch performances from the shore. During the first few weeks of July, the village of Lockenhaus competes for attention with its Chamber Music Festival. The world renowned violinist, Gideon Kremer, and the local parish priest, Josef Herovic, are the joint patrons of this village festival where the audience and performers casually mingle during intermissions. Even though Haydn's birth-house is in Rohrau, Lower Austria, Burgenland claims him as its greatest musical son. One residence of his most important patrons, the Hungarian Esterházys, can be visited in Eisenstadt *(Schloss Esterházy)*, and one can see where Haydn frequently conducted his own works. Haydn's house from 1766 to 1778 is just a stone's throw from the palace in a small street which bears his name, Haydngasse 21, and the composer is buried in a local church. (Next to Haydn, Burgenland claims Franz Liszt as its second contribution to the world of music.) Burgenland is also famous for its wines — the tart white *Grüner Veltliner* and the hearty red *Blaufränkischer* predominate — which are frequently served at vintners' homes, the *Heurigen*, seasonally adapted to entertain.

Styria

TI: Steiermärkischer Landesfremdenverkehrsverband, Herrengasse 16, Landhaus, A-8010 Graz, tel. (03 16) 70 31-0
LM: Steiermärkisches Landesmuseum Joanneum, Neutorgasse 45, Graz

Northern Styria is Alpine and industrial. The Dachstein, Niedere Tauern, Eisenerz, and Hochschwab ranges provide for spectacular scenery and popular recreational areas. The Erzberg, a mountain which has been completely terraced in the process of exploiting its rich iron ore desposits, is the source of nine-tenths of Austrian iron ore and, at the same time, a symbol for Upper Styria's industries concentrated in the Mur and Mürz valleys. Styria, however, has the reputation of being Austria's greenest province. The mountains and forests in the North are complemented by farmers' fields in the lowland South, which are bracketed to the east and west by rolling hills. One of Styria's most imposing symbols of its tradition as a border-land is the Riegersburg Castle which successfully withstood numer-· ous attacks by the Hungarians and Turks. The latter are also responsible for a typically Styrian dish, *Türkensterz*, a "Turks' mash," a cornmeal porridge which tastes much better than it sounds. *Schilcher*, a red wine with the color of a rosé, pressed from grapes cultivated only in southern Styria, is a tart and earthy Styrian drink enjoyed best with *Verhackertes* — a spread made of finely chopped, smoked bacon — on dark bread. The *Weinstrassen*, "wine-roads," one of them through the areas where *Schilcher* is produced, are beautiful drives, in summer or fall in particular. Graz, provincial capital and Austria's second largest city, is the site of Austria's biggest festival dedicated to contemporary arts and the avant-garde, the "Styrian Autumn" held annually from September through mid-November. The Armory *(Zeughaus)* in Graz has a collection of 29,000 weapons dating from the 16th to the 19th centuries and is the largest and best preserved installation of its kind in the world. In and out of town men wear the *Steireranzug,* the "Styrian suit" — originally a peasant design — made of heavy gray wool with green lapels on the jacket and a green stripe down the side of each trouser leg. This traditional Styrian dress is so popular beyond the province's borders that it almost can be called typically Austrian.

Upper Austria

TI: *Oberösterreichisches Landesfremdenverkehrsamt, Schiller-strasse 50, A-4010 Linz, tel. (0732) 663 021*
LM: *Oberösterreichisches Landesmuseum Francisco-Carolinum, Museumstrasse 14, Linz*

Emperor Francis Joseph spent his summer vacations in Bad Ischl in the *Salzkammergut,* an Alpine "lake district" shared by Upper Austria, Styria, and Salzburg. A visit to the Imperial Villa *(Kaiservilla)* is just as important as seeing the home of the operetta composer associated with this famous spa, Franz Lehár *(Lehármuseum).* Bad Ischl also sponsors annual "Operetta Weeks" each summer from July through mid-August. (However, many Upper Austrians feel that these imperial and operettic attributes are artificial imports rather than genuine provincial traits.) The *Salzkammergut* has been famous for its salt since ancient times. A visit to one of the local salt mines is a fascinating adventure, but not recommended for claustrophobics. Hallstatt, a picturesque village clinging to the mountainsides which plunge into Hallstätter Lake, is simply beautiful and also the site of important prehistoric archeological finds. Linz, the largest industrial center in Austria and home of the nationalized VOEST steelworks, is the site of an annual festival dedicated to the works of Upper Austria's most famous composer. The International Anton Bruckner Festival runs from September through mid-October, and it is complemented annually by Ars Electronica, a festival for electronic music and multi-media happenings. Linz has its own pastry made of apricot jam and ground almonds, the *Linzertorte*. Typically Upper Austrian food reflects the province's agricultural regions in or north of the Danube Valley. *Geselchtes mit Griessknödeln*, smoked ham with semolina dumplings — semolina is a by-product of grinding wheat to make flour — and a hard apple cider called *Most* are good examples of rural, provincial fare. A schnaps made from plums, pears, and apples called *Obstler* helps one digest after dinner. Many people associate the Baroque monasteries of St. Florian or Kremsmünster with Upper Austria. Although it is not typical for the province, people interested in contemporary history may visit the former Nazi concentration camp of Mauthausen (located not far from Linz) which also has a museum and a series of commemorative monuments for its victims.

Carinthia

TI: Landesfremdenverkehrsamt Kärnten, Kaufmannstrasse 13, A-9021 Klagenfurt, tel. (0 42 22) 5 54 88
LM: Landesmuseum für Kärnten, Museumgasse 2, Klagenfurt

During the thirties, the construction of the *Grossglockner* Road from Carinthia to Salzburg through the Alps was a pioneer task, and the views it offers today's motorists are breathtaking. For a panoramic view of Austria's highest mountain, the 12,457 ft. *Grossglockner*, drive up to a terrace called the *Franz-Josef-Höhe,* keeping in mind that cyclists cover the same stretch on bikes each year during the annual *Tour d' Autriche.* However, for a view from Carinthia's most famous castle, Hochosterwitz, you will have to walk. It is perched on a stone butte and can only be reached by following a serpentine path that goes through a series of fourteen gates. A visit to the province's lakes like the *Millstätter See, Ossiacher See,* and *Wörther See,* is less strenuous, but the scenery is just as beautiful. These lakes are great attractions in summer, and Carinthia has a reputation for being the most clement province in Austria. The province's largest annual festival, the "Carinthian Summer," also provides for ample musical refreshment. Many of its concerts are held in a Baroque monastery church a stone's throw from the shores of the *Ossiacher See.* However, the Cathedral of Gurk, one of Austria's most famous and beautiful Romanesque churches, has its own series of concerts, too. Speaking of churches, *Kirchtagssuppe,* "church-day soup," is a Carinthian specialty which used to be served only at annual church festivals. It has a base of broth, sweet and sour cream, five kinds of meats, and delicate spices, and nowadays can be enjoyed daily. Another local treat is *Kasnudeln,* literally "cheese-noodles," which are not noodles at all, but generous helpings of cheese wrapped in a noodle dough and then boiled. *Kletzennudeln* is a dessert prepared the same way with a filling made of small pears. Most of the province's Slovene minority live in the shadow of the *Karawanken,* a dramatic range of limestone Alps which provide a strong geological contrast to the mountains in the north of province. The farmers of southern Carinthia distill a plum schnaps called *Slivovitz* which is typical for Styria and Yugoslavia as well.

Salzburg

TI: Salzburger Land Tourismus-Gesellschaft, Alpenstrasse 96, A-5033 Salzburg, tel. (06 62) 20 506
LM: Salzburger Museum Carolino-Augusteum, Museumplatz 6, Salzburg

In Salzburg, it is important to distinguish between the provincial capital and its rural hinterland. Mozart's birth-house in the *Getreidegasse* is a pilgrimage site for people from all over the world. A local puppet theater, the *Marionettentheater*, has fascinating performances of Mozart operas, and it is sometimes attended as a consolation for those people who could not get tickets for Salzburg's annual Summer Festival held from the end of July to the end of August — a musical event with a global reputation second only to Bayreuth's Wagner Festivals. Salzburg's annual Easter Festival, however, makes up for this shortcoming by partially concentrating on Wagner. The *Hohensalzburg* Castle dominates the cityscape, and a visit to the Baroque Hellbrunn Palace, built by one of Salzburg's prince-archbishops outside the city, is well worthwhile. The palace park has a famous set of fountains adorned with mechanical figures which occasionally spray unsuspecting visitors. *Salzburger Nockerln* is typical fare for the city — a rich, fluffy pile of meringue baked golden brown — but this type of sophistication is not symptomatic of Salzburg's countryside. *Mus*, a wheat and rye porridge, used to be standard fare for farmers and lumberjacks, and *Kasnocken*, small dumplings made out of a cheese and flour dough, are perhaps more typical today. Farmers have their own festivals, too. Religious holidays like Christmas, Epiphany, Easter, and Corpus Christi, as well as important events in the farmer's calendar like the end of winter or driving cattle down from their Alpine pastures in the fall, are festivals of folkloric flair in all of Austria's Alpine regions. *Loden* wool, now a world-renowned Austrian material, has humble Alpine origins, and much of it is produced in Salzburg today. The province's natural attractions range from the *Wolfgangsee* in the *Salzkammergut* over the *Eisriesenwelt* (Ice Giant's World), a series of ice caves and caverns near Werfen, which also has an imposing castle, to the *Grossvenediger*, Austria's second highest peak. Which part of Salzburg is most beautiful has been a topic of debate among the inhabitants of its different regions for centuries.

Tyrol

TI: Tiroler Fremdenverkehrswerbung, Bozner Platz 6, A-6010 Innsbruck, tel. (0 52 22) 2 07 77
LM: Tiroler Landesmuseum Ferdinandeum, Museumstrasse 15, Innsbruck

Which Tyrol should you visit? Tyrol is one land divided by two states into three regions. The revision of the Austrian-Italian border in 1919 separated East Tyrol from North Tyrol by making South Tyrol part of Italy, and North Tyrol tend to overshadow these two less renowned but equally Tyrolean regions. Innsbruck hosted the Winter Olympics in 1964 and 1976, and these events definitely contributed to the province's reputation as a winter sports haven, but to assume that North Tyrol's Alps are more representative or more beautiful than the Dolomites of East and South Tyrol does injustice to Tyrol's diversity. East Tyrol's involuntary isolation makes it one of the most untouched regions in the Alps, and in South Tyrol you can enjoy the warm air and influences of the Mediterranean along with a glass of local Tyrolean red wine. Visits to East Tyrol's regional capital of Lienz or South Tyrol's Bozen are less common but just as important as a stop in Innsbruck, where people go out of their way to see the Renaissance Ambras Castle with its museums or visit the *Hofkirche*. In this church, Emperor Maximilian, who preferred Innsbruck over Vienna, had a gigantic burial monument erected during the 16th century which has 28 over-life-sized bronze figures portraying his predecessors. (It is one of those quirks of history that Maximilian is buried in Wiener Neustadt, Lower Austria.) Tyroleans themselves define Tyrol valley by valley, and one is more beautiful than the next. For inhabitants of the Zillertal, yodelling and folk music accompanied by zithers and harps are typically Tyrolean. Processions of masked dancers which go back to ancient, pagan, Alpine rites in Imst, Nassereith, or Telfs can make the same claim just like the passion plays held in villages like Thiersee and Erl. Reflections of Alpine traditionalism, festivals of pagan and Christian folklore abound in the Tyrolean calendar, and these events are particularly common in remoter regions where traditional Tyrolean cooking is also at its best. Even though the *Knödel* (dumpling) with various stuffings is common throughout Austria, Tyrol has managed to elevate *Knödel* to the status of a Tyrolean national dish. *Tiroler Graukäse*, "gray cheese" served with oil, vinegar, and onions, or *Gröstel*, a fried potato dish served with cold cabbage salad, are also typical fare. This kind of down-to-earth food provides a strong contrast to the sophistication which prevails in Tyrol's ski areas, which, much to the consternation of adjoining provinces, have á reputation for being the best in Austria.

Vorarlberg

TI: Landesfremdenverkehrsverband Vorarlberg, Römerstrasse 7/I, A-6901 Bregenz, tel. (0 55 74) 2 25 25
LM: Vorarlberger Landesmuseum, Kornmarkt 1, Bregenz

Many Austrians themselves never make it to Vorarlberg in the course of their lifetimes, but those who do have two ways of getting there. Driving through the Arlberg Tunnel is quickest. A drive over the Hochtannberg Pass is more time-consuming, but spectacular. The former route is recommended for people who do not particularly like serpentine mountain roads; the latter winds up through the mountains and then down through the forests to the Rhine Valley, *Bregenzerwald*, Lake Constance, and the provincial capital of Bregenz. From the end of July until the end of August, Bregenz hosts Austria's second largest music festival, and one of the festival's attractions is the performance of operettas or musicals on the *Seebühne*, a stage erected over the waters of Lake Constance which allows the audience to view from shore. A boat ride on Lake Constance is just as typical for Vorarlberg as Lech and Zürs, villages so well known for their ski areas that they can compete with the ones in Tyrol, but it is also important to see the valleys of Vorarlberg in between these aquatic and alpine extremes. The road from Bregenz to Feldkirch is lined with castles built by the Monforts, the medieval rulers of the region, and their stronghold, Schattenburg Castle, still dominates the cityscape of Feldkirch. Bludenz, farther up the road, is a perfect point of departure for exploring the Alpine way of life because it is at the junction of five valleys. People interested in tracing ancient Raeto-Roman traditions go to the Montafon Valley, whereas those with a predilection for Alamannian-Swiss influences go up into the *Grosses* and *Kleines Walsertal*. It is most interesting, of course, to be able to compare both. *Gerstensuppe*, a hearty soup made with barley, is typical for the Montafon region, but many Vorarlbergers would call *Käsknöpfle,* literally "cheese buttons," the provincial dish. The buttons are small dumplings, covered by a layer of cheese, then more dumplings, and more cheese until the pot is filled. The cheese of Vorarlberg incidentally is as good as anything the Swiss produce, or, as some of the natives maintain, even better. Due to the importance of Swiss influences, Eastern Austrians accuse Vorarlberg of being Austria's only canton. The Vorarlbergers themselves, however, have a much more balanced view: they represent the best of both worlds.

Recommendations for Further Reading

There are a tremendous number of books that fall into that broad category called *Austriaca*. The following suggestions concentrate on topics related to 19th and 20th century Austria assuming that they are most accessible and of greatest interest to general readers. People interested in specialized topics should consult the selected bibliography following this section.

Richard Rickett's *A Brief Survey of Austrian History* is, in spite of some minor flaws, the best short historical introduction available; however, people with a special interest in Vienna should read *Vienna – The Past in the Present: A Historical Survey* by Inge Lehne and Lonnie Johnson. The standard work on Austrian history, Robert A. Kann's *A History of the Habsburg Empire: 1526–1918*, is much too scholarly and detailed for general readers, who are well advised to start with Ernst Wangermann's readable and richly illustrated *The Austrian Achievement: 1700–1800*, Edward Crankshaw's *Maria Theresia*, or his *The Fall of the House of Habsburg*, if they want good introductions to the 18th and 19th centuries respectively. Karl Stadler's *Austria*, unfortunately out of print, is the best survey of the 20th century, and the Austrian Federal Press Service publishes a handy little book dealing with contemporary Austria called *Austria: Facts and Figures*.

People interested in life and times of Emperor Francis Joseph have their choice among biographies dealing with family tragedies. Frederic Morton's bestseller, *A Nervous Splendor: Vienna 1888–1889*, focuses on the events leading up to the suicide of Crown Prince Rudolph and vividly captures the spirit of the times as does Brigitte Hamann's *The Reluctant Empress: A Biography of Empress Elisabeth of Austria*. Gordon Brook-Sheperd's *The Archduke of Sarajevo: The Romance and Tragedy of Franz Ferdinand of Austria* traces the personal and political misfortunes preceding the assassination that began World War I.

Turn of the century Vienna is the topic which has attracted most attention recently, and among the wealth of publications Carl E. Schorske's provocative and prize-winning collection of essays, *Fin de Siècle Vienna: Politics and Culture*, simply cannot be overlooked. William Johnston's *The Austrian Mind: An Intellectual and Social History, 1848–1938*, a valuable reference for anyone interested in intellectual history, is nicely complemented by Bruce Pauley's *The Habsburg Legacy: 1869–1939*, a history which covers the collapse of the empire and the First Republic.

George Clare's *Last Waltz in Vienna: The Destruction of a Jewish Family, 1842–1942*, which interweaves a lucid historical narrative with a family history and an autobiography, covers the darkest chapters of contemporary Austrian history. *Modern Austria*, a collection of articles edited by Kurt Steiner, offers a comprehensive overview of Austria's development since World War II, which is rounded off nicely by *Austria Since 1945*, edited by William E. Wright.

Selected Bibliography

Andic, Hellmut, *Der Staat, den keiner wollte* (Molden: Vienna, 1968; 2nd revised edition, Goldmann: Munich, 1984)

Benedikt, Heinrich, ed., *Geschichte der Republik Österreich* (Verlag für Geschichte und Politik: Vienna, 1954)

Birnbaum, Karl, and Hanspeter Neuhold, ed., *Neutrality and Non-Alignment in Europe* (Braumüller: Vienna, 1982)

Botz, Gerhard, *Wien vom Anschluß zum Krieg* (Jugend und Volk: Vienna/Munich, 1978)

Cronin, Audrey K., *Great Power Politics and the Struggle over Austria 1945–1955* (Cornell University Press: Ithaca/London, 1985)

Czeike, Felix, *Geschichte der Stadt Wien* (Molden: Vienna/Munich/Zurich, 1981)

Heer, Friedrich, *Der Kampf um die österreichische Identität* (Böhlau: Vienna/Cologne/Zurich, 1981)

Hiscocks, Richard, *The Rebirth of Austria* (Oxford University Press: London, 1953)

Hofmannsthal, Hugo von, *Reden und Aufsätze II: 1914–1924* (Fischer: Frankfurt, 1979)

Kann, Robert A., *A History of the Habsburg Empire: 1526–1918* (University of California Press: Berkley, 1974)

Kindermann, Gottfried-Karl, *Hitlers Niederlage in Österreich: Abwehrsieg 1934* (Hoffmann und Campe: Hamburg, 1984)

Kleindel, Walter, *Österreich – Daten zur Geschichte und Kultur* (Ueberreuter: Vienna/Heidelberg, 1978)

Lehne, Inge, and Lonnie Johnson, *Vienna – The Past in the Present: A Historical Survey* (Österreichischer Bundesverlag: Vienna, 1985)

Leser, Norbert, and Richard Berczeller, *Als Zaungäste der Politik* (Jugend und Volk: Vienna/Munich, 1977)

Leser, Norbert, *Zwischen Reformismus und Bolschewismus: Der Austromarxismus als Theorie und Praxis* (Europaverlag: Vienna, 1968: 2nd edition, Böhlau: Vienna/Cologne/Graz, 1985)

Lutz, Heinrich, and Helmut Rumpler, ed., *Österreich und die deutsche Frage im 19. und 20. Jahrhundert* (Oldenbourg: Munich, 1982)

Luza, Radomir, *Austro-German Relations in the Anschluss Era* (Princeton

University Press: Princeton, 1975)

Luza, Radomir, *The Resistance in Austria* (University of Minnesota Press: Minneapolis, 1984)

Maier-Bruck, Franz, *Das Große Sacher Kochbuch – Die österreichische Küche* (Schuler Verlagsgesellschaft: Munich, 1975)

Meissl, Sebastian, Klaus-Dieter Mulley, and Oliver Rathkolb, ed., *Verdrängte Schuld – Verfehlte Sühne: Entnazifizierung in Österreich 1945–1955* (Verlag für Geschichte und Politik: Vienna, 1986)

Musulin, Stella, *Austria: People and Landscape* (Faber and Faber: London, 1971)

Nick, Rainer, and Anton Pelinka, *Bürgerkrieg – Sozialpartnerschaft: Das politische System Österreichs 1. und 2. Republik* (Jugend und Volk: Vienna/Munich, 1983)

Pauley, Bruce, *Hitler and the Forgotten Nazis: A History of Austrian National Socialism* (MacMillan: London, 1981)

Pauley, Bruce, *The Habsburg Legacy: 1867–1939* (Holt, Rinehart, and Winston: New York, 1971; reprint Krieger, 1981)

Pelinka, Anton, *Windstille: Klagen über Österreich* (Medusa: Vienna/Munich, 1984)

Pisa, Karl, *Österreich: Land der begrenzten Möglichkeiten* (Deutsche Verlagsanstalt: Stuttgart, 1985)

Rauchensteiner, Manfried, *Der Krieg in Österreich 1945* (Österreichischer Bundesverlag: Vienna, 3rd edition, 1985)

Rauchensteiner, Manfried, *Vom Limes zum "Ostwall"* (Österreichischer Bundesverlag: Vienna, 3rd edition, 1985)

Rosenblit, Marsha, *The Jews of Vienna 1867–1914: Assimilation and Identity* (State University of New York Press: Albany, 1983)

Stadler, Karl R., *Austria* (Ernest Benn Ltd.: London, 1971)

Stadler, Karl R., *Österreich 1938–1945 im Spiegel der NS-Akten* (Herold: Vienna/Munich, 1966)

Steiner, Kurt, Fritz Fellner, and Hubert Feichtelbauer, ed., *Modern Austria* (SPOSS: Palo Alto, 1981)

Steiner, Kurt, ed., *Tradition and Innovation in Modern Austria* (SPOSS: Palo Alto, 1982)

Stiefel, Dieter, *Entnazifizierung in Österreich* (Europaverlag: Vienna/Munich/Zurich, 1981)

Stourzh, Gerald, *Geschichte des österreichischen Staatsvertrages 1945–1955* (Styria: Graz/Vienna/Cologne, 2nd revised edition, 1980)

Sully, Melanie, *Continuity and Change in Austrian Socialism* (Columbia University Press: New York, 1982)

Sully, Melanie, *Political Parties and Elections in Austria* (C. Hurst & Co.: London, 1981)

Wagner, Georg, *Österreich – Zweite Republik: Zeitgeschichte und Bundestradition*, 2 vol. (Österreichischer Kulturverlag: Vienna, 1983)

Weinzierl, Erika, and Kurt Skalnik, ed., Österreich 1918–1938: Geschichte der Ersten Republik, 2 vol., (Styria: Graz/Vienna/Cologne, 1983)
Weinzierl, Erika, and Kurt Skalnik, ed., Österreich: Die zweite Republik, 2 vol. (Styria: Graz/Vienna/Cologne, 1972)
Wright, William E., ed., Austria since 1945 (Center for Austrian Studies – University of Minnesota: Minneapolis, 1982)
Zöllner, Erich, and Therese Schüssel, Das Werden Österreichs (Österreichischer Bundesverlag – Verlag für Geschichte und Politik: Vienna, 6th edition, 1985)
Zweig, Stefan, Die Welt von Gestern: Erinnerungen eines Europäers (Fischer: Frankfurt, 1984)

Picture Credits

If one picture is worth a thousand words, a caricature is worth two thousand; therefore, special thanks to Gustav Peichl (Ironimus) for putting his works at the publisher's disposal.

The following people were also exceptionally helpful in finding or providing pictures for this book: Bernhard Denscher, Siegwald Ganglmair, Gerhard Jagschitz, Marion Powers, Manfried Rauchensteiner, Gexi Tostmann, and the staff of the Österreichische Nationalbibliothek, Bildarchiv, Vienna.

INDEX